America's next "great awakening" will be broadly ecumenical and led by scholar-pastors such as R. T. Kendall. This book draws on a biblical vision that is true to the author's confessional roots and yet open to the ways in which the Holy Spirit is leading Christians to unite in healing the wounds of our nation and world.

—CARDINAL TIMOTHY M. DOLAN
ARCHBISHOP, NEW YORK

In the face of our national chaos, this book gave me hope and peace.

—JOY STRANG
CFO, CHARISMA MEDIA
LAKE MARY, FLORIDA

R. T. Kendall gives America a road map in *We've Never Been This Way Before*. It seems that we have lost our way in here in the West, and R. T. Kendall's book is a trumpet blast to our country, saying, "This is the way, walk in it" (Isa. 30:21). Proverbs 25:11 reminds us that there is truth and then there is timely truth. *We've Never Been This Way Before* is timely truth for every believer, especially at a time when truth has fallen in the streets. Like a great physician, R. T. Kendall's book diagnoses the chaotic times in which we are living in America. It then proceeds to give the prescription that nothing but an awakening can rescue our nation. I am grateful that finally someone has written with a prophetic voice, a theological mind, and the heart of a father in the faith an important word that our country needs to hear today.

—TIM DILENA
SENIOR PASTOR, TIMES SQUARE CHURCH
NEW YORK CITY

W9-BXX-340

R. T. Kendall's books are timeless, but this book is *on time*. He brings truth from God's Word for how to live in this chaotic world, how to be used of God, to look forward to our greatest days, to prepare our hearts for the greatest awakening the world has ever known, and to "fix our eyes on Jesus, the author and perfecter of our faith" (Heb. 12:2, BSB).

—RICKY SKAGGS
RECORDING ARTIST
MEMBER, GRAND OLE OPRY HALL OF FAME

From the moment I saw the title of this book, I was gripped. *We've Never Been This Way Before* is a heart-stirring and thought-provoking interpretation of the signs of our times. Too often we consider the kindness of God but fail to recognize His sternness. Too often we focus on grace but pass by essential themes such as judgment and consequences. In this powerful read, my wise friend R. T. rectifies this—bringing us a serious and challenging word for the unprecedented moment we find ourselves in. And though he teaches much on judgment and repentance, his message is ultimately one of redemptive grace and future hope. This exceptional book is a message for our times—a clarion call to the US church and beyond.

—MATT REDMAN
WORSHIP LEADER, SONGWRITER

We were lost in the back roads of rural southwestern Pennsylvania. It appeared that our guidance system in our SUV seemed more aware of it than we were when we heard it say, "You have come to the end of all known information." At first we couldn't believe our ears, and then we burst into laughter. We had never been that way before.

There is an incredible statement that God makes to His people in the Book of Jeremiah. God expresses astonishment at the magnitude of their sinfulness. He declares that they "have built the high places of Baal to burn their sons in the fire as burnt offerings to Baal, a thing which I never commanded or spoke of, nor did it ever enter My mind" (Jer. 19:5, NASB). The four issues addressed in this carry the same measure of astonishment for many of us. It would be totally appropriate to read this book on your knees since its message will provoke a desperate need to seek God. Elihu reminded Job and his friends, "Age should speak, and multitude of years should teach wisdom" (Job 32:7, NKJV). I hope that this book will be used by the Holy Spirit to galvanize each of us into the kind of action that will touch the very heart of God.

—BISHOP JOSEPH L. GARLINGTON SR.
FOUNDING PASTOR, COVENANT CHURCH OF PITTSBURGH
PRESIDING BISHOP, RECONCILIATION! MINISTRIES
INTERNATIONAL

Precious gems, insights, and answers are in store for everyone who reads this timely book, *We've Never Been This Way Before*, by R. T. Kendall. God has His hand on this beautifully God-inspired book for a divine purpose during the present situation in our world. He wants His body to be free, free to minister, free to witness, free in body, mind, and spirit.

R. T. has demonstrated in writing not only how God is using civil unrest and COVID-19 to wake America up but how we must return to being one nation under God. Many books will address our current issues, but this book is so simple and explanatory in its delivery that every person who reads it will understand God's part in this crisis and what each person needs to carry them through this time of upheaval.

The biblical examples and R. T.'s experiences as a pastor will encourage each reader in their spiritual walk and will convince anyone that our God is God and there is no other! This book is a must for every person who is experiencing fear, unrest, and a feeling of no hope. Best of all, this book will give solid biblical answers for how God is using these circumstances in our world to change us and prepare us for His will to be accomplished.

—MARILYN HICKEY
EVANGELIST, BIBLE TEACHER

Dr. Kendall's wake-up call is timely and timeless. We are in the crosshairs today, and we must return to God. Read the book and share it with friends.

—ALVEDA C. KING
EVANGELIST; DIRECTOR, CIVIL RIGHTS FOR THE UNBORN

We've Never Been

This Way
Before

R.T. KENDALL

🔥 CHARISMA HOUSE

Visit the author's website at rtkendallministries.com.

Library of Congress Cataloging-in-Publication Data:
An application to register this book for cataloging has been submitted to the Library of Congress.
International Standard Book Number: 978-1-62999-950-0
E-book ISBN: 978-1-62999-951-7

While the author has made every effort to provide accurate internet addresses at the time of publication, neither the publisher nor the author assumes any responsibility for errors or for changes that occur after publication. Further, the publisher does not have any control over and does not assume any responsibility for author or third-party websites or their content.

20 21 22 23 24 — 987654321
Printed in the United States of America

To Paul and Sandy

CROSSING RIVERS

We have never been this way before,
So how then will we know the way to go?
Trusting that the Lord our God will be our guide,
We will cross the river to the other side.

So be strong and courageous, put your armor on, be brave.
He has come to the rescue of the ones He came to save.
To the land of milk and honey, we are following the Lamb.
He will give to us the victory, every place our feet set down.

I will do amazing things among you,
I will set your feet on solid ground.
No weapon of the enemy shall prosper,
My Name will be exalted through this land.
—KIERAN GROGAN[1]

CONTENTS

FOREWORD

O<small>N</small> G<small>OOD</small> F<small>RIDAY</small>, April 10, 2020, I stood in the Oval Office of the president of the United States. I was honored to be asked to pray a prayer after the president shared some remarks about the holiday. This was an amazing moment in my life; my research shows that millions listened and agreed with the prayers offered at that event.

Two days before, the first day of Passover, I went to the White House for what would prove to be a dry run for Friday's prayer. Two trips to the White House in one week! This was quite an accomplishment for a minister raised in the African American ghettoes of Cincinnati, Ohio. During those encounters and discussions, I was asked by the president if I was ever nervous before I spoke. I remarked that I was nervous right then because He was the most powerful man in the world.

During those visits, I got tested for COVID-19 for the first time. Next, I met the famed Dr. Anthony Fauci and Dr. Deborah Birx, and they remarked that African Americans had a disproportionate infection rate with the virus. I had been fasting and praying intermittently for nearly one month. I realized that President Trump understood that his presidency and the lives of millions were in God's hands—not just his hands. I could see the weight of the presidential office upon him. He remarked that he had to make the most important decisions of his life in that moment. He was right. Therefore, he directly beseeched the wisdom and blessings of God through prayer. He had summoned me as a representative of Christ's church to invoke a blessing or to implore the Almighty to release His protective power.

These are truly perplexing times. There are obvious anomalies in what's going on in our nation. How can I live in one of the most religious counties in the DC area, but it has the highest COVID-19 infection rate in my home state of Maryland? Why is the racial division in our nation coming to the forefront at this time? Clearly God is humbling our nation and giving us an opportunity to change. The biggest lesson that I learned from the Good Friday prayer is that God has His own agenda.

We've Never Been This Way Before gives the best biblical perspective I have heard of where we are today. R. T. Kendall attempts to help us negotiate these difficult waters by answering the question "Where is God in all this?" This book calls us back to the pages of the Bible. It calls us back to the first and most important steps to real repentance, renewal, and cultural reformation. Reverend Kendall makes the case that our nation's most pressing problems— COVID-19 and racial tensions—have a spiritual root. These problems must be addressed through both practical and spiritual strategies.

Our largest churches often focus more on man's needs than God's direction and directives. While the Bible clearly tells us not to lean to our own understanding, most Americans are caught up in our own understanding. This means we focus on opinions about our national direction, our strategies for defeating COVID-19, and the origins or or cures for our ethnic conflicts. The average US Christian believes that we can use strategy or technology to solve any problem before us. If strategy is all we need, where is our need for God?

Over the years, we have begun to veer away from truly trusting God to trusting our intellect and our wealth. As a result, church leaders in other nations of the world are wondering whether the US church is investing in political power instead of spiritual power. R. T. Kendall is clearly advocating for spiritual power. He is calling the church to think biblically and to return to the Lord's mercy and goodness.

There are two scriptures that will help any reader to receive practical personal and corporate direction from this book. The first scripture is Amos 3:7, which says, "Surely the Lord GOD does nothing unless He reveals His secret counsel to His servants the prophets" (NASB). The "secret counsel" referred to here is actually the Lord's "training secret." Said another way, if God is making a point, prophetic voices give instruction and direction.

R. T. Kendall is giving a personal and practical guide to how we should respond to what God is doing in our world today. Therefore, this work is extremely prophetic. Historically, our biblical prophets call God's people back to righteousness and holiness.

Unfortunately many people want to hear predictions or prognostications at times like these. The Bible, however, points us to a second scripture about prophetic messages such as this book. The scripture is so straightforward and profound that it is often overlooked. First Corinthians 14:3 says, "But the one who prophesies speaks to people for their strengthening, encouraging and comfort" (NIV).

This amazingly well-written and engaging book does exactly what prophetic books should do. It encourages us to walk with God during this difficult time. It presents lofty theological truth in bite-size, digestible pieces. It is a must-read in this season.

As I read the book, I was warned, confronted, and corrected by the power of the Word. At the end of the process, I was given the gift of perspective and hope. I believe that the church is going to lead the way in solving America's four-hundred-year race problem. It is also going to address the call for health care reform in the twenty-first century. These are "love thy neighbor" issues that must be solved because of Christian convictions and leadership. In the biblical account of Passover three benefits came forth as the nation of Israel was released:

1. They came out with silver and gold; there was an economic reset for God's people.

2. There were no feeble ones among them. (People who were affected by other diseases were healed.)

3. They had supernatural guidance into the Promised Land against the tenth plague.

When we have fully obeyed R. T. Kendall's prophetic message, similar benefits to Israel's Passover will be manifest in our lives.

Nearly fifteen years ago I was diagnosed with terminal cancer—given only a 10–15 percent chance of living for five more years. Without the diagnosis, a great treatment plan, and the power of God released through prayer, I would be singing in the heavenly choir. Reverend Kendall has done for us what my doctor did for me. He has given us a spiritual diagnosis for our nation's woes, offers a treatment plan, and gives us the ability to cooperate with God's vision for America.

—BISHOP HARRY R. JACKSON JR.
SENIOR PASTOR, HOPE CHRISTIAN CHURCH,
BELTSVILLE, MARYLAND
PRESIDING BISHOP, INTERNATIONAL COMMUNION OF
EVANGELICAL CHURCHES

PREFACE

RECENTLY CHARISMA HOUSE asked me if there was anything on my heart that related to the coronavirus crisis that is all over the world. "Yes," I replied, "as a matter of fact, there is." What has been on my heart is unfolded in this book. But I had not thought of writing such a book until they asked me. Of all the books I have written, two stand out when it comes to thoughts flowing quickly: *Holy Fire*, which my publisher asked that I write, and this one—*We've Never Been This Way Before*.

The divine instructions to the children of Israel as they were preparing to enter Canaan, "You have never been this way before" (Josh. 3:4, NIV) gripped me over twenty years ago when I preached through the Book of Joshua at Westminster Chapel. Those words came to my mind during the tumultuous times of the first half of 2020 and came to my mind immediately when my editor contacted me. This book has been written in the shortest period of time of any of my books and yet flowed with the most ease of any I have written.

That does not mean you have to take every word seriously! I'm sure it could be improved on if we had more time!

I want to express thanks to Dan Cathy, CEO of Chick-fil-A. Though I have not met him, he has kindly permitted me to quote him as I do in chapter 5. Although I did not need to ask him for legal reasons since what he said is in the public domain, I wanted to make sure he still stood by what he said—that America needs to repent over its racism.

It is my conviction that America is under judgment—for at least four reasons: (1) its racism, (2) legalizing abortion, (3) approving of same-sex marriage, and (4) theological liberalism in many churches. But I am hopeful—or I would not have written this book.

My thanks to my editor, Debbie Marrie, for inviting me to write this book and share my views concerning the current crises in America. A huge thank-you to Joy Strang for taking the time to read my manuscript and to her husband, Stephen, the owner of Charisma, for giving me a broader ministry ever since we retired from Westminster Chapel in 2002. And thanks to my wife, Louise, my best critic, who has been gifted with wisdom as she has read all that follows.

This book is being dedicated to our beloved friends Paul and Sandy Berube of the Gate City Church in Nashua, New Hampshire.

—R. T. KENDALL
HENDERSONVILLE, TENNESSEE
JULY 2020

INTRODUCTION

You have never been this way before.
—JOSHUA 3:4, NIV

W E ARE IN two major crises at the moment. Both are unprecedented. It might be said that we have been given a double whammy in the year 2020: (1) the coronavirus crisis—which is a natural phenomenon, and (2) sudden civil unrest that has its origin in racial prejudice. It is impossible to say now which of these may be more difficult for our nation.

The Lord not only knows perfectly where we have been but equally knows where we are going. He realizes when we are facing the unprecedented. The fact that He graciously gave this word to the children of Israel—"You have never been this way before"—reveals how loving and compassionate the God of the Bible is. I cannot imagine a more comforting or reassuring word than this word to the children of Israel. God said this to them as they prepared to lead the children of Israel into the Promised Land—the land of Canaan.

First of all, as I write this, we are still in what is probably the most significant natural crisis in the history of the whole world. It is called the coronavirus crisis because the outbreak of this virus has led to many people contracting the disease known as COVID-19. *CO* stands for corona. *VI* stands for virus. *D* stands for disease. 2019 refers to the year it first emerged, according to the World Health Organization (WHO). It is scary. Troubling. Even terrifying.

1

We are all vulnerable. Not only has our way of life been at stake; our very lives are at stake. Our health is at stake. Our finances are at stake. The safety of our loved ones is at stake. What we have been familiar with all our lives will almost certainly never be quite the same again. The new normal is that nothing will be normal as we have known it. Virtually every person in the world is in some way touched by this.

And yet, secondly, when it appeared that the danger of COVID-19 was beginning to subside, another crisis suddenly emerged, causing some to think that it may be more impacting than what had already struck the nation with fear. It happened overnight when a White police officer in Minneapolis, Minnesota, put his knee on the neck of a helpless George Floyd, a Black man aged forty-six, for several minutes until he died. The news of this spread all over the world in twenty-four hours. Never in my lifetime have I known such outrage as was caused by this incident. Violent protests broke out in almost every large city. This was followed by peaceful protests that may lead to political and social change in many places.

I chose the title of this book, based on God's words in Joshua 3:4, because they so aptly relate to our times. We are facing life with *what* has never been but also heading *where* we have never been.

God did not have to give this word to Joshua for him to pass on to the children of Israel. Joshua already knew that. But why did God order it to be said? It was a reminder that He was totally involved with what was going on in the lives of the children of Israel. He raised Moses to lead Israel and sent the ten plagues to Egypt. He led Israel to cross the Red

Sea on dry land and then destroyed the armies of Pharaoh by drowning them in the Red Sea. It was God who sent supernatural food—the manna—to provide for them in the desert for forty years.

But now that era was over. The time had come at last for Israel to enter into their promised inheritance. However, their able leader, Moses, was not allowed to enter Canaan. This made the future more challenging. Before he died, the baton had been passed to Joshua. The buck now stopped with him. But when Moses died, God assured Joshua, "Just as I was with Moses, so I will be with you. I will not leave you or forsake you" (Josh. 1:5).

Therefore, for God to bother to say to the children of Israel, "You have never been this way before," revealed how intimately tied God was to the people of Israel and how tenderly and carefully He looked after them. Indeed, it shows He had got right into the people's skin. Just as Jesus, our great High Priest, would be touched by our weaknesses thousands of years later (Heb. 4:15), so the eternal God had already tenderly demonstrated His love to ancient Israel. God wanted Joshua to know that He knew exactly what all were feeling; He knew everything that was in their minds. As the psalmist would later say,

> O LORD, you have searched me and known me!
> You know when I sit down and when I rise up; you
> discern my thoughts from afar. You search out my
> path and my lying down and are acquainted with
> all my ways. Even before a word is on my tongue,
> behold, O LORD, you know it altogether.
> —PSALM 139:1–4

Israel was the Lord's treasured possession (Deut. 7:6). Why did God feel this way about Israel? The only reason: because He loved them. But why? Not because they were numerous. Not because they were good. Not because they were worthy. "It was not because you were more in number than any other people that the LORD set his love on you and chose you, for you were the fewest of all peoples, but it is because the LORD loves you" (Deut. 7:7–8). So why did God love Israel? *Because He did.*

Why does God love any of us? *Because He does.* It is not because of our goodness but due to His purpose and grace (2 Tim. 1:9). That means we are utterly unworthy of His mercy and grace.

As Israel had to go forward without Moses, so do we have to face the future with new leaders. The revered leaders of the past—both spiritual and political—are no longer with us. Our parents, old friends, and people we have somehow leaned on for wisdom are gone. We feel daunted. Scared. Almost overwhelmed.

But it is equally true: as God was with Moses, so will He be with us. He does not want us to lean on the past. "Say not, 'Why were the former days better than these?' For it is not from wisdom that you ask this" (Eccles. 7:10).

Today we are involuntarily outside our comfort zones. You and I did not decide to go outside our comfort zones. We were not consulted. That was decided for us. With little or no warning. Like it or not, we are all suddenly having to cope with the new and different.

I used to be a door-to-door vacuum cleaner salesman. It was not where I wanted to be. It was a painful era. I was thrust outside my comfort zone; owing to deep debt I brought on myself (because I did not know how to handle money), I had to take a most unprestigious job that would pay the bills. Those were difficult days. Although that was over fifty years ago, hardly a week goes by to this day that I do not dream of struggling to sell vacuum cleaners to people who were not remotely in the market for such. I woke up recently recalling the line I used to get into a house to demonstrate my product. It was so humbling and embarrassing. While my fellow students at my old college in Nashville were pastoring churches, I would go up to a house, ring the doorbell, and say: "Hello. I am R. T. Kendall. I have come to show you something new and different for your home." I did this for over six years.

The present crises—the new and different—are not for sale. Money will not change things. The pain of COVID-19 makes my old job of selling vacuum cleaners—even if doors were slammed in my face—now seem like sheer comfort and joy. The continual threat of violence anywhere—owing to someone doing or saying something unwise—is as unsettling as the fear of getting a fatal disease.

As for my previously mentioned point that we were not consulted whether we would allow these crises to come our way, the question is, Who did decide this? As for COVID-19, who brought this? The World Health Organization? China? The US military? Some government in the world? God? As for the sudden unrest troubling the nation owing to the cruel act of a police officer, who is to blame? Racial prejudice? Weak political leadership? Or is God responsible?

The question that Christians raise—or the question non-Christians will put to us is, Where is God in all this? I loved what I heard Cardinal Timothy Dolan of New York say on

Fox News speaking of the coronavirus crisis: "God is right in the middle of it."[1] Yes! However, that could either mean that God caused it or that He decided to jump in and get involved in it after it came. But where was God in the more recent national crisis? Is God judging America? We need to think seriously about this and other questions, and I will discuss these further in this book.

Some say that Christianity has no answer for COVID-19— nor should it have an answer. This is sad. Of course we have an answer! Furthermore, as we will see, God *expects* us to ask why all this has happened. We would be obscurantists if we didn't ask! As Christians we believe two infallible truths: (1) creation is by God alone (Gen. 1), and (2) that Jesus Christ upholds all things—*everything,* including the entire universe—"by the word of his power" (Heb. 1:3). We are therefore bound to ask, "Did God *cause* these two crises? Or did He consciously and voluntarily *permit* them?"

Some well-meaning people say that Satan caused what has happened, since they say God would *never* be responsible for anything bad. Nonsense. Listen to these words:

> "Does disaster come to a city, unless the LORD has done it?...I struck you with blight and mildew; your many gardens and your vineyards, your fig trees and your olive trees the locust devoured; yet you did not return to me," declares the LORD. "I sent among you a pestilence after the manner of Egypt; I killed your young men with the sword."
>
> —AMOS 3:6; 4:9–10

We have heard lately of several serious fires in Australia. Locusts in Africa. Who is to say that God would not do this?

Some of us choose to believe what is pleasant because it makes us feel good. Listen to Isaiah:

> I form light and create darkness; I make well-being and create calamity; I am the LORD, who does all these things.
>
> —ISAIAH 45:7

These passages don't seem to reconcile with most American pulpits and American preaching today. And yet "there is a way that seems right to a man, but its end is the way to death" (Prov. 16:25). It "seems" right to say God only causes good things and good feelings, and if it is bad, it must be from the devil. While the role of Satan must be taken into account, God certainly has indeed caused bad things—over and over again.

We must ask, "Where is God in what is happening in 2020? Is Satan more able than God?" We must look at the two crises separately and not paint all that has happened with a broad brush.

Dr. Martyn Lloyd-Jones (1899–1981) taught me a theological lesson from the account of Moses at the burning bush. Moses saw a bush on fire, but the bush did not burn up. This was strange, so Moses decided to go directly to this burning bush to figure out what caused a bush to be on fire and yet not be consumed. As he approached the burning bush, God intervened and said, "*Stop*. Do not come any closer. Take off your shoes. You are on holy ground" (my paraphrase—see Exodus 3:5).

Not only that; Moses hid his face, for "he was afraid to look at God" (Exod. 3:6). Moses became willing not to know but instead to fear God—to let God be God. This goes to show that God will not allow us to figure out what He does not want us to figure out. There are some things God wants to remain a mystery. Thus there are some things that God does not *allow* us to figure out. My conclusion from this account: *the difference between what God causes and what He permits is holy ground. Let us take off our shoes and worship.*

In a word: God will let us go so far in understanding His ways but no further. Some of us are in danger of allowing reason or logic rather than Scripture to control our conclusions. The truth is, we must stay with Scripture and not try to figure everything out. We must take off our shoes and worship. We must be willing to not know everything. You may be sure of this: God will not allow us to figure out what He does not want us to figure out. If we push to figure out what God does not want us to figure out—just because we want things to be neat and tidy—we will end up accepting not only what is not true but even what is bizarre.

The burning bush example certainly applies to the coronavirus crisis. We must not be hasty in trying to get on top of understanding its origin. We must take off our shoes.

However, the current crisis of unrest in America is easier to figure out. This is because being a nation "under God" and having a Declaration of Independence and a Constitution that were born with a view to honoring the Creator God, we are compelled to believe that God is involved. There is no doubt that the hand of God has been on America. The refrain of the hymn is true:

America! America! God shed His grace on thee!
—Katharine Lee Bates (1859–1929)[2]

Is God at the bottom of the current unrest in America? Yes.

Consider the question "Who crucified Jesus?" Do you have a view as to who crucified Jesus? There are at least six views—each of them being true:

1. Pontius Pilate did it. Being the Roman governor, the Jews needed his authority and permission to crucify Jesus. Pilate ordered the crucifixion (Matt. 27:26; Mark 15:15; Luke 23:25; John 19:16).

2. The Roman soldiers did it. Indeed, they were the men who literally did the heinous job of crucifying Jesus (John 19:23).

3. The Jews did it. They were the ones who persuaded Pilate to order Jesus' crucifixion and said to him, "His blood be upon us and our children!" (Matt. 27:25).

4. Satan did it. The devil entered into Judas Iscariot (John 13:2, 27), who then betrayed Jesus. Indeed, Satan thought that he was the mastermind of the crucifixion. Had Satan and the rulers of this age known what Jesus' crucifixion would lead to, they "would not have crucified the Lord of glory" (1 Cor. 2:8).

5. You and I did it. Oh yes. It was our sins that led Jesus to Golgotha. Never forget this: we did it. As John Newton put it in his hymn, "I saw my

sins His blood had spilt, and helped to nail Him there."[3]

6. God did it. Isaiah saw it hundreds of years in advance—Jesus was "smitten by God"; it was the "will of the LORD to crush him; he has put him to grief" (Isa. 53:4, 10).

The Scriptures also say, quoting from Peter's sermon on the day of Pentecost, that the crucifixion was carried out "according to the definite plan and foreknowledge of God" (Acts 2:23). Peter also said that Jesus was crucified and "killed by the hands of lawless men" (Acts 2:23). This perspective was stated again when the earliest church was being persecuted. They prayed, lifting their voices together, noting that Herod and Pontius Pilate, along with the Gentiles and the people of Israel, did "whatever your hand and your plan had predestined to take place" (Acts 4:28).

The crucifixion of Jesus is the most evil act of human beings in world history. Nothing compares to it. It was an example of infinite injustice.

That said, then, remember that God was responsible for what happened on Good Friday. The previous examples also show how more than one explanation might be offered before we get God's verdict—that He is sovereign and all-powerful. It shows that there was more than one explanation for what happened—that is, until God stepped in to give the ultimate cause of Jesus' crucifixion.

Could that be true concerning the latest crisis in America? Yes. The breath of Satan has been all over the violence—the killing and the damage done to jobs and stores, further crippling the economy. Satan is right in the middle of it. Just as the devil entered Judas, so has he masterminded the recent bloodshed. Killing George Floyd was an act of Satan. This is what initiated the second crisis of 2020. But we learn from the Book of Job that Satan could go no further than what God allowed. And never forget the main lesson to be learned from the Book of Job. He confessed to God, "No purpose of yours can be thwarted" (Job 42:2).

I choose to believe—believe with all my heart—that God has not utterly taken His hand off our nation. The same is equally true of the United Kingdom. If He has left us bereft, there is absolutely nothing we can do about it. But I also believe that if these crises are yet one more way that He is trying to get our attention, then there is hope. As God was ultimately responsible for the injustice done to His Son on Good Friday—though Satan was also showing his ugly hand in nearly all of it—there is reason to believe that He is up to something very wonderful nowadays.

> For my thoughts are not your thoughts, neither are your ways my ways, declares the LORD. For as the heavens are higher than the earth, so are my ways higher than your ways and my thoughts than your thoughts.
>
> —ISAIAH 55:8–9

We are not commanded to figure out everything. But we can figure out some things. In any case, we are commanded to worship.

God says, "I am with you. I will never leave you or forsake you. You have never been this way before."

That comforting and undoubted truth drives me to my knees to ask God for mercy. Those words, "You have never been this way before," are the prelude to a miracle—the parting of the Jordan River and the Israelites entering into their promised inheritance. Unless God opened up those waters, their feet never would have walked on that soil or ground. We need for God to open the waters so we can go forward as the people of God into a territory where we've never been before.

I genuinely believe that is coming. Take the first step with me as we walk where we've never walked before.

Chapter One

WHERE WE *HAVE* BEEN BEFORE

He chose David his servant and took him from the sheepfolds.
—PSALM 78:70

Be still, my soul: thy God doth undertake to
guide the future as He has the past.
—KATHRINA VON SCHLEGEL (1697–1797),
TRANSLATED BY JANE BORTHWICK (1813–1897)

G OD KNOWS WHERE we have come from. He knows perfectly our past—our sins, our failures, our successes, our weaknesses, all influences on us, our spiritual pilgrimage, our limits. He knows everything. Things we have forgotten, God remembers. According to Paul, God chose the time and place of our birth. This means He chose our parents.

> He made from one man every nation of mankind
> to live on all the face of the earth, having deter-
> mined allotted periods and the boundaries of their
> dwelling place.
>
> —ACTS 17:26

Have you ever wondered why you were born in the twentieth century and not in 500 BC? Have you wondered why you were not born in Mongolia or Ecuador?

This much I know: "The LORD has made everything for its purpose" (Prov. 16:4). "The LORD has made everything for his own purposes" (NLT). "The LORD has made all for Himself" (NKJV).

I don't know why I was born in Kentucky. I have heard my parents tell how they met and how they prayed for a son. My parents were godly Christians. They were not perfect. I lost my temper at the age of six when I burned my tongue on hot oatmeal, accusing my mother of making things too hot. She said to me, "When you get sanctified, God will take that temper out of you." This was not helpful; it made me angrier.

My first schoolteacher had some weird teaching methods. I believe that she was responsible for my inability to read well or enjoy reading. She would stand behind me as I read from a book in front of the class and immediately shake my shoulders when I mispronounced a word, making me cry in front of everybody. She scared me to death. I am sure that is mainly why I still have to fight to concentrate to keep my eyes on a sentence—whether I am reading a secular book or the Bible.

David, son of Jesse, not only became king of Israel but was Israel's greatest king. David was also a poet, a musician, a warrior—indeed a military genius and the writer of many psalms. Not only was he chosen from the sheep pens, but his father vastly underrated him. The great prophet Samuel had come for dinner to anoint the next king. Jesse had eight sons and introduced Samuel to seven of them. He did not even let young David know that the legendary Samuel was on the premises. It did not cross Jesse's mind that David was the man God had chosen to be the next king of Israel. But as God said to Samuel, "The LORD sees not as man sees: man looks on the outward appearance, but the LORD looks on the heart" (1 Sam. 16:7).

That should encourage many of us. You may not be well

bred, highly cultured, or educated; you may be underesti-
mated by your employer, school teacher, or parents. You
may feel sure that there is little chance that God would use
someone as insignificant and unqualified as you. I reply:
you are the very person God deems as qualified to do the
next thing He needs. You may be the last person that those
who know you would expect to be tomorrow's man or
woman. Your friends and siblings may underestimate you.
Indeed, they may be jealous of you. David's brothers were
jealous of him (1 Sam. 17:28).

David was a man after God's "own heart" (1 Sam. 13:14;
Acts 13:22). That means having a heart that yearns to please
God: to obey Him. It does not mean you are perfect. David
was not perfect. (See 2 Samuel 11.) God does not use perfect men and women (there aren't any!); He uses forgiven
men and women. A good example: Peter who preached the
inaugural sermon on the day of Pentecost. Six weeks before
Peter proved to be a coward and denied even knowing Jesus.
That made Peter the most unlikely candidate to be used of
God. But, after he repented, he proved to be powerful and
faithful, even writing two books in the New Testament.

Your unhappy past might convince you that God can
never use you. You fear that any plan God may have had for
you has now been set aside. After all, you have spent time
in prison. You had an abortion. You married the "wrong
man" or the "wrong woman." You were unfaithful to your
spouse. You mishandled money, even stole money. You
ruined another life by what you said about them—which
was even untrue. You were not kind to your parents. Or you
have been even a worse parent than they. God knows *where*
you have been. He knows *what* you have been.

You have decided that you do not have a brilliant future because of your lack of education. You aren't sure you have a worthwhile gift. As for being well-connected? No chance. You are a nobody.

The God of the Bible enjoys taking a nobody and turning him or her into a somebody.

Reuben Robinson was born January 27, 1860, in White County, Tennessee. He was tongue-tied, quit school at the age of nine, and could neither read nor write. When he was twenty years old, a stranger took an interest in Reuben and invited him to a tent meeting, where there was preaching every night. Reuben allegedly replied something like this: "I don't know where it is or what it is, but because you have expressed such a love for me, I will go."

He went and listened to a sermon. At the end of the sermon an altar call was given, inviting people to come and kneel and confess their sins. His friend suggested that Reuben go forward to kneel and pray. He replied, "I don't know where it is or what it is, but I will go." He prayed and asked God to save him. He was converted. Reuben shortly thereafter felt called to preach even though he was tongue-tied and largely uneducated.

He became known as Uncle Buddy Robinson and not only became a legend in my old denomination, the Church of the Nazarene, but reportedly led over 250,000 souls to Christ. My parents loved to boast that they hosted Uncle Buddy in their home shortly after they were married.

God looks at the heart. I find that encouraging to this day. Surprising as this may seem to some readers, I don't feel I have accomplished all that I want to do. I will tell you why. When I was seventeen years old, I was befriended by my

US senator from Kentucky, John Sherman Cooper (1901–1991). I was allowed not only to watch the Senate debate but also to go into the office of the Senate president (who is also the vice president of the United States). While I was in his office, someone said, "Why don't you sit in the president's chair?" I did. Then someone said, "Everyone who sits in that chair makes a wish, so make a wish!" I have no idea why I did this, but I quietly bowed my head and said, "Make me a great soul winner."

That prayer is unanswered. I have written a few books, preached in a lot of places, and led a few people to Christ. But not many. There was a time when I aspired to be a great theologian. For a while I wanted to prove certain points of view—that is, until I had a vision on the steps of Westminster Chapel, having followed Arthur Blessitt to the streets to speak to passersby. I had a vision of a pilot light—a light that stays lit day and night, as in a cooker or an oven. I knew in my heart of hearts that God was calling me to be a one-to-one evangelist. Until then I rationalized that I did my duty as an evangelist by preaching the Gospel from the pulpit every Sunday. It's easier to preach to hundreds than it is to speak to one person, especially a stranger. I died a thousand deaths. My desire (it was a vain desire, to be honest) to be a great theologian was upgraded. I became willing to be a personal soul winner. Having the aforementioned vision, our Pilot Light ministry was born. In the words from one of the verses of the hymn "I Will Praise Him,"

> Tho' the way seems straight and narrow,
> All I claimed was swept away;

My ambitions, plans and wishes,
At my feet in ashes lay.
                    —MARGARET J. HARRIS (1865–1919)[1]

Ever since that life-changing evening in Buckingham
Gate I have aspired preeminently to be an evangelist—a
winner of souls—who preaches the historic Gospel with
power and authority. Until I go to heaven, I will hope with
all my heart to see that prayer I offered at the age of seventeen answered.

God can say to any of us, "You have never been this
way before," because He knows exactly and totally where
we have been before, what we have done, what we have not
done, and where we are at the moment.

HOW TO LET GO OF THE PAST

Are you ashamed of your past? Do you worry about past
sins? Maybe you believe you have failed people and let
them down. Perhaps you think you have failed God. Do
you know whether your sins have been forgiven? Do you
know whether—if you were to die today—you would go to
heaven? You may say that you don't believe the Bible, but
I will quote one verse from it that you will totally agree
with: "It is appointed for man to die" (Heb. 9:27). We are
all going to die. You may not like the second part of that
verse, which says after you die, you face "judgment." This
means you will stand before God. So will I. Like it or not,
you and I will have to give an account of ourselves. It will
not be fun. It will be the scariest day of our lives. And yet
you may know in advance how your case will be tried on
that Judgment Day. You could call it "settling out of court."

You need to know two things. The first is that God sent His Son, Jesus Christ, into the world to live a perfect life in your behalf and then die for you. He called it fulfilling the law (Matt. 5:17), meaning living out the Ten Commandments in thought, word, and deed sixty seconds a minute, sixty minutes an hour, twenty-four hours a day, every day of His life. He did this for you—that is, as your substitute, since you cannot live like that.

We are sinners, but Jesus never sinned (Heb. 4:15). At the age of thirty-three He was crucified. He hung on the cross for approximately six hours, enduring the worst kind of pain ever known to humankind. While He was on the cross, all our sins were imputed to Him as though He had committed them Himself. He took the blame for our sins. That is actually why He came to this world. That was the purpose. Not only that; God punished Jesus that day for what we did. The blood He shed satisfied the wrath and justice of God. He was the *propitiation* for our sins (Rom. 3:25; 1 John 2:2). That word means that Jesus turned the Father's wrath away from us.

The second thing you need to know is that you must acknowledge that you are a sinner, be sorry for your sins, and then *transfer the trust* you have had in yourself to what Jesus did for you by His sinless life and sacrificial death. This is called saving faith. It is what gets you to heaven. It means you must abandon any hope in your good works to save you—no matter how great these works might have been.

If indeed you believe this way in your *heart*, congratulations. Only the Holy Spirit could cause you to feel this way.

Here is a prayer I suggest you say to God to bring this home and give you assurance that you are truly saved.

> *Lord Jesus Christ, I need You. I want You. I know I am a sinner. I am sorry for my sins. Thank You for dying on the cross for my sins. Wash my sins away by Your blood. I believe You are God in the flesh and that You were raised from the dead. I welcome Your Holy Spirit into my heart. As best as I know how, I give You my life. Amen.*

Perhaps you are merely a nominal Christian. This means you accept certain Christian truths in your head but not your heart. You are possibly trusting in your baptism, your church membership, or your being born into a Christian home. If the truth be told, your honest confidence is in your good works. This means you have never been converted; you are not saved. I would urge you to read again what I wrote previously. Ask God to enable you to feel sorry for your sins. Either you feel this way, or you don't.

Perhaps you are a sleepy Christian. This means you have been genuinely saved but have grown cold. You have not been faithful in living the Christian life. You have accepted social practices you once rejected. You have lost a sense of outrage of practices that go right against Holy Scripture. You have swept these things under the carpet and have refused to think about them. The Bible does not thrill you as it once did. Time alone with God in prayer has been almost nonexistent. When someone lovingly approaches you about these things, you become defensive and annoyed. These things said, recent crises have sobered you. God is beginning to get your attention. I would therefore urge you to go back to reading your Bible. Go back to praying as you once did, and seek God with all your heart. I suggest this prayer:

> *Heavenly Father, I am sorry I have wandered from You. I am sorry for my indifference and failure to pray and read Your Word as I once did. Thank You for Your wake-up call. Thank You for getting my attention at last. I am sorry for the way I have lived, for thoughts I have embraced, and for accepting things that grieve Your heart. Please forgive me. Wash my sins away by Your blood. Thank You for 1 John 1:9, which says if we confess our sins, You are faithful and just to forgive our sins and cleanse us from all unrighteousness. Thank You that You have not utterly left me. I welcome the Holy Spirit in the measure I once enjoyed. In Jesus' name, amen.*

God has had His hand on you all along. He knows where you have been. He knows where you are going and that you have never been this way before.

Chapter Two

THE FAMILY SECRET

*And we know that for those who love God all
things work together for good, for those who
are called according to his purpose.*
—ROMANS 8:28

*If you have money, power, and status today, it is due to the
century and place in which you were born, to your talents
and capacities and health, none of which you earned. In
short, all your resources are in the end the gift of God.*
—TIMOTHY KELLER

I HAVE USED ROMANS 8:28 almost entirely alongside my
name in the last sixty-five years when I sign a letter or a
book. I lean on it all the time. If you knew how often I have
messed up over the years—and still do more often than I
wish—you would understand why I love this verse. What
a promise! It means what it says, that everything that has
happened in the past will work for good. It does not say
that good things work together for good. Good things don't
need to work together for good. They are already good! The
promise means that things *less than good* work together for
good.

This verse mirrors a larger principle. There are two polar
opposite worldviews when it comes to the issue here: existentialism versus a theodicy. *Existentialism* is a hopeless
philosophy that says there is no rhyme nor reason for our
existence. There is no purpose in what happens. As for evil
and wickedness, such just happens; you will never know

why. Wrong! There is also a *theodicy*—the view that there is a purpose and meaning to life. Our Creator God is a God of purpose. God will one day wind up things and clear His name and magnify the honor of His Son. "So that at the name of Jesus every knee should bow...and every tongue confess that Jesus Christ is Lord, to the glory of God the Father" (Phil. 2:10–11).

Paul does not say that everything that happens is good. There is nothing good about a plane falling from the sky. There is nothing good about a hurricane or tornado. There is nothing good about an accident that leaves one injured or crippled. There is nothing good about losing your sight or hearing. There is nothing good about losing your job. There is nothing good about COVID-19. There is nothing good about a wicked policeman putting his knee on a helpless Black man's neck until he dies. There is nothing good about violent protesting that results in damaging stores and taking away one's job. There is nothing good about being hated or rejected because of the color of your skin.

You may ask, "What about my sins? Does Romans 8:28 cover my sins as well?" I answer: "If Romans 8:28 does not cover my sins, it has little meaning for me at all. My most painful regret is sins I have committed and the guilt that followed such. So does Romans 8:28 cover my sins? *Yes.* "All things work together for good" to those who love God and are the called according to His purpose. What a wonderful, comforting verse!

Yes, God knows where we have been. He sympathizes with our foolishness, the offhanded comment, the friendship turned sour, the hasty decision that turned out to be so bad, our hurts, and all that is in our shameful past.

OUR FREE PASS

Why is Romans 8:28 the *family* secret? For two reasons.
First, not all believe this! Not all are expected to believe
this. Only those in the family believe this. You may say, "I
don't believe for one moment that all things work together
for good." Paul answers: "I never thought you would. It was
not meant for you; it is for those in the family." That is why
he says, "*We* know. You may not, but we do."

Second, the promise is true only for those who love
God, "for those who are called according to his purpose."
Things certainly don't work together for good for everybody. Certainly not. Those outside the family experience
the opposite: chaos, unrest, trouble, confusion, hopeless-
ness. Things don't work together for good for the unsaved.

Caution: the fact that something works together for
good in the end does not mean that it was right at the time.
The husband may say to his wife, "See there, it shows I
was right." It may not show that at all. God made it work
together for good, but this does not justify you!

Another caution: it is for those who *love* God—present
tense. This promise does not apply to those who once loved
God but no longer demonstrate love for Him. As long as
people live in a sleepy state, as we saw previously, they
need not expect to have everything working together for
good. Hardly. But for those who repent of their wayward-
ness and *love* God, it puts God to work for them! After all,
it is He who makes this happen. Things don't automatically
work together for good. Things work together for good
because God *makes all things work together for good*.

But how do we know this? We have found it to be

true! When Paul says "we know," he uses the Greek word *oidamen*. This refers to knowledge of a well-known fact: what goes up must come down; water is wet; the sun is hot; there are twenty-four hours in a day. No one disputes these facts. That is the word Paul uses—"we know," from *oida*. Every Christian can testify to the truth of this verse. The good may not be discovered by tomorrow afternoon, but in a while we see that God causes the past—whatever is in it— eventually to turn out for good.

Romans 8:28, then, is a verse that refers to the *past*. God knows where we have been. It is not a verse that gives someone carte blanche to live irresponsibly. It refers to the past, not the future. Romans 8:28 is God's way of saying, "I don't want you to feel guilty." It is God's way of saying, "As for the past, leave it with me; watch what I do."

God will take a tongue-tied, uneducated man named Reuben and make him a legend. God can take a young shepherd named David who had no idea God was on his case and turn him into one of the greatest men of all time. God loves taking a nobody and making him or her a somebody.

God doesn't want you to help Him. Don't say, "I must make sure that what I did works for good; therefore I must do this." If you try to make something work together for good, it will get worse—every time. God does not want your help; He wants to get all the glory. It is the same principle regarding vindication. If we vindicate ourselves—or even try to do it a tiny bit—God will back off and let you see what a mess you will make without Him.

We are all on the brink of a new chapter in our lives. What is ahead presents a more significant challenge than we have known. God knows this. He sympathizes and shows the way forward. The same God who has guided us in the past will not forsake us. And as for the past, God knows exactly where each of us has been. The family secret is our free pass to a guilt-free past. That said, we can know that the same God who ensures that all things work together for good is the God who promises to stay close by us as we go where we've never been.

He will not desert us.

Chapter Three

THE GLORY

As soon as you see the ark of the covenant of the LORD
your God being carried by the Levitical priests, then
you shall set out from your place and follow it.
—JOSHUA 3:3

...looking to Jesus, the founder and perfecter of our faith.
—HEBREWS 12:2

MANY MOVIEGOERS WILL be familiar with the film *The Raiders of the Lost Ark*. It is supposedly linked to the same ark of which I have been speaking. Although the movie is based entirely upon fantasy, there was nothing superstitious about the original ark of the covenant. God totally designed it. The Israelites constructed it in the desert during their forty years of sojourn there. It was a chest made of acacia wood, two and a half cubits in length, one and a half cubits in breadth, and one and a half cubits in height. The lid, a slab of pure gold, became the mercy seat in the most holy place, or holy of holies, in the ancient tabernacle. "There I will meet with you," God said (Exod. 25:22). The high priest would enter into the most holy place once a year (on the Day of Atonement) and sprinkle blood of an animal on the mercy seat to make atonement for the sins of the people. The two tablets of the Ten Commandments, a jar of the manna the people ate in the desert, and Aaron's rod that budded were placed inside the ark.

The ark was a symbol of the glory of God. Indeed, it was more than a mere symbol. The immediate presence of

God was in some way attached to the ark. Years later the Lord struck seventy men of Beth-shemesh dead "because they looked upon the ark of the LORD," possibly looking inside it (1 Sam. 6:19). Years after that a man named Uzzah was struck dead by touching it (2 Sam. 6:6–7). One of the highest moments of his reign was when King David successfully brought the ark into Jerusalem; he was overjoyed (2 Sam. 6:12–15).

The word *glory* comes from the Hebrew *kabodh*, meaning heaviness or weightiness, high stature or importance. The Greek word for glory is *doxa,* which means praise. Its root meaning is opinion. The glory of God is the dignity of His will or opinion. The glory is the nearest you get to trying to describe God's essence. It is the sum total of all His attributes. There are many attributes of God: omnipotence (He is all-powerful), omniscience (He is all knowing), and omnipresence (He is everywhere). He is holy, loving, just, and sovereign. But the word *glory* encompasses all these attributes. Stephen, when testifying before the Sanhedrin, called Him "the God of glory" (Acts 7:2). Moses longed to see God's glory most of all but was allowed only to see His "back" (Exod. 33:18–23). "I am the LORD; that is my name; my glory I give to no other" (Isa. 42:8). King Herod put on his royal robes and enjoyed the people shouting that his voice was the voice of God and not of a man. The angel of the Lord struck Herod down "because he did not give God the glory" (Acts 12:23).

When we truly glorify God, it is because we focus entirely on Him, give Him alone the praise and thus prioritize His opinion—His will. God has a will of His own. It is not our duty to change it but to find out what it is and honor it. When we pray the petition "Your will be done, on earth as it is in heaven" from the Lord's Prayer (Matt. 6:10), we affirm that the will of God is always being carried out perfectly in heaven. There is no rebellion there—whether among the angels or the sainted dead. We are praying for that to be the case with us; we are praying that we are completely submissive to His will. We must never forget that God has His own opinion as to what is best for us. We are fools if we do not follow it. There is great reward for those who seek His opinion, get it, and follow it. His opinion is found in Holy Scripture.

> The law of the LORD is perfect, reviving the soul; the testimony of the LORD is sure, making wise the simple; the precepts of the LORD are right, rejoicing the heart; the commandment of the LORD is pure, enlightening the eyes; the fear of the LORD is clean, enduring forever; the rules of the LORD are true, and righteous altogether. More to be desired are they than gold, even much fine gold; sweeter also than honey and drippings of the honeycomb. Moreover, by them is your servant warned; in keeping them there is great reward.
>
> —PSALM 19:7–11

The common people of Israel almost certainly had not laid their eyes on the ark of the covenant. But on the day chosen for them to say goodbye to the desert and head toward Canaan, they were allowed to see the ark. However,

> There shall be a distance between you and it, about 2,000 cubits in length. Do not come near it, in

order that you may know the way you shall go, for
you have not passed this way before.

—JOSHUA 3:4

The ordinary people, namely all the tribes except the
Levites, were to keep a certain distance from it—two thousand cubits, which is one thousand yards—for two reasons.
The first is to show respect for the ark. To dignify it. Israel
was taught from early on to demonstrate a solemn deference for the ark. This is a hint to all of us not to be overly
chummy or buddy-buddy with the Lord. Although God
certainly does want us to enjoy intimacy with Him, even
knowing Him as Abba (Rom. 8:15)—the Aramaic equivalent of daddy—for some of us it is the only side of God
we ever see when we worship Him. Consequently, we miss
experiencing the majesty and awe of God. The absence
of His glory is sadly reflected in so many religious songs
written in our time.

Second, the distance of one thousand yards was stipu-
lated so that everybody could always see the ark. For had
this distance not been set as it was, only those who happened to be near the ark would have been able to see it.
They needed to see not only the glory of Israel but where
they were going. They would not be traveling aimlessly.
Chosen Levites carried the ark. Poles that fit through loop-
holes on the sides of the ark enabled these men to move it
without touching it.

Since the children of Israel had never been this way
before, they would need to keep their eyes on the ark to feel
safe and secure. They would feel safe and know that they
were not being left behind as long as they could see the

ark. The writer of Hebrews had precisely this in mind when he referred to "looking unto Jesus, the founder and perfecter of our faith" (Heb. 12:2). This is addressed to Hebrew Christians who had been urged to come into their promised inheritance—and not repeat the fatal error of ancient Jews who had come short of the promise.

OUR GOD IS A JEALOUS GOD

An integral part of the glory of God is His jealousy. God is up front about His jealousy. He makes no apology for this. "The LORD, *whose name is Jealous*, is a jealous God" (Exod. 34:14, emphasis added). He gave this as the reason for the second commandment:

> You shall not make for yourself a carved image, or any likeness of anything that is in the heaven above, or that is in the earth beneath, or that is in the water under the earth. You shall not bow down to them or serve them, for I the LORD your God am a jealous God, visiting the iniquity of the fathers on the children to the third and the fourth generation of those who hate me, but showing steadfast love to thousands of those who love me and keep my commandments.
>
> —EXODUS 20:4–6

Our heavenly Father being a jealous God is a wonderful truth for which all of us should be deeply thankful. If you are a parent, it is the way you feel about your children. You are jealous for their safety, security, good health, and success. That is precisely the way God feels about us.

Keeping your eyes on Jesus—the glory of God—will

keep you out of trouble. It will keep you from regrettable mistakes. As long as you keep your eyes on His glory, you will know the next step to take. You will be safe. You also will be enabled to see miracle after miracle—the equivalent of crossing the Jordan on dry land, watching the walls of Jericho fall, and conquering every enemy God puts in your path.

You have never been this way before. But you have the privilege of seeing the glory all the way. One of the most magnificent and comforting promises is this:

> For the LORD God is a sun and shield; the LORD bestows favor and honor. No good thing does he withhold from those who walk uprightly.
>
> —PSALM 84:11

The sun provides light and warmth. A shield is protection from anyone or anything that would harm you. He promises to bless you and exalt you. Nothing good will be withheld from you but bestowed upon you. Walking uprightly does not mean you are perfect; it means you want to keep your eyes on His glory.

Are you worried about your future? Are you concerned about how you will survive the double whammy that has fallen on America? Are you afraid to die? Are you threatened by the unknowns of an altogether different future? You have never been this way before, but your peace of mind is guaranteed if you have a love for the glory of God.

Jonathan Edwards (1703–1758) said that the one thing Satan cannot produce in us is a love for God's glory. The flesh cannot come up with it, your friends cannot pass it on to you, and money cannot buy it. It is not inherited from the best parents in the world. The most excellent education will not enable you to love God's glory. So if the thought of keeping your eyes on God's glory causes your heart to leap, congratulations! Only God can put that there!

THREE THINGS GOD'S GLORY WILL DO

A fast track by which you can know God's ways is to grasp various ways the glory of God is to be understood and applied in the Bible. Embracing the glory of God does three things for you, and I will explain them now.

1. It makes you feel unworthy to be a Christian.

You are conscious of the goodness of God, knowing that it is sheer grace that is responsible for your conversion. Yes, you made a choice. Yes, you repented. Yes, you put your trust in Jesus' blood. But how did you do this?

The great Charles Spurgeon (1834–1892) found himself in a Methodist church one day and began to ask himself this question: "How did you come to be a Christian?" He thought about it for a moment when suddenly he said, "I saw that God was at the bottom of it all."[1]

The Gospel is so designed that God gets all the glory for our salvation. But we must be willing to not take credit for the way God may be pleased to use us. President Ronald Reagan (1911–2004) had a plaque on his desk in the Oval Office that read "There is no limit to what a man can do or where he can go if he does not mind who gets the credit."[2] This is the same principle that lies behind the Gospel of grace; it is the same principle that will lead us to where we've never been. Keeping their eyes on the ark enabled the children of Israel to reach the land of their inheritance.

Keeping our eyes on Jesus will protect us, prosper us, and provide for us in these uncertain times.

2. It will keep you from a feeling of entitlement.

When Moses asked to see God's glory, he was given specific lessons about God's ways. God said to him, "I will be gracious to whom I will be gracious, and will show mercy on whom I will show mercy" (Exod. 33:19). This lets you know that if God is gracious to you, you ought to be very, very thankful. It is because Jesus has chosen you. What He said to His disciples He now says of you: "You did not choose me, but I chose you" (John 15:16). We are all like Nathanael, who exclaimed to Jesus, "How did you know me?" Jesus replied: "Before Philip called you, when you were under the fig tree, I saw you" (John 1:48).

The inevitable feeling of realizing that God has been on our case is *gratitude*. All we can do is say, "Thank You, Lord." It is humbling. We feel so in awe. We ask why, and God answers, "Don't try to figure it out. Just take off your shoes and worship."

The opposite of gratitude is a feeling of entitlement. A sense of entitlement is widespread in America generally and among many Christians particularly. A vision of God's glory will make us feel unworthy and grateful. As we will see, knowing how easy it is to forget, God taught the children of Israel to be thankful.

3. The revelation of God's glory convinces you how real God is.

There is nothing so rewarding as the immediate and direct presence of God. The children of Israel had experienced the provision of the manna in the wilderness. It was supernatural food. They had seen how God delivered them from enemies during these years—from Sihon, king of the Amorites, and Og, king of Bashan—and how the visible glory of God led them. "The cloud of the LORD was on the tabernacle by day, and fire was in it by night, in the sight of all the house of Israel throughout all their journeys" (Exod. 40:38).

The ark of the covenant became the visible manifestation by which the children of Israel knew they were led by God and were not being deceived. All they had to do was keep their eyes on the ark. The pillars of cloud and fire would now come to an end. Eating the supernatural manna was now coming to an end. Indeed, nothing would be "normal" again; the new normal would be that nothing would be normal as they had known it.

To put it another way, they would now have to live entirely by faith. As long as we can *see* the visible presence of God, little or no faith is needed. As long as we can eat supernatural food, little or no faith is required. Hebrews 11 is a description of men and women who did what they did by faith: believing God without seeing the evidence (Heb. 11:1). You and I are now being called to do in our day what they did in theirs. The challenge before us is formidable. We have never been this way before. We all are going to find out very soon whether our faith is real, genuine, the real deal.

We have an opportunity to walk in the steps of those described in Hebrews 11. Each of them had in common that they were not able to repeat what the previous person of faith did. Noah could not repeat Enoch's being translated to heaven. Abraham could not do what Noah did; instead of building an ark, Abraham went out and did not know where he was going (Heb. 11:8). And so it was with every single person described in Hebrews 11.

That is where you and I are today. Not only do we have to go where *we've* never been; we are going where *nobody* has been. Of course, it sounds terrifying. But we have the same God that all those had who have gone on before us.

All you and I need to do in our double whammy era is keep our eyes on Jesus. "For God, who said, 'Let light shine out of darkness,' has shone in our hearts to give the light of the knowledge of the glory of God in the face of Jesus Christ" (2 Cor. 4:6). As the chorus puts it, let us turn our eyes upon Jesus and "look full in His wonderful face."[3]

How wonderful that the God of glory is in charge of taking us where we have never been. All we need is to keep our eyes on Him.

Chapter Four

IS AMERICA UNDER JUDGMENT?

*Woe to those who call evil good and good evil, who
put darkness for light and light for darkness, who
put bitter for sweet and sweet for bitter!*
—ISAIAH 5:20

*God the all-terrible! King, who ordainest great winds thy
clarions, lightnings thy sword, show forth thy pity on high
where thou reignest; give to us peace in our time, O Lord.*
—HENRY F. CHORLEY (1808–1872)

*In those days there was no king in Israel. Everyone
did what was right in his own eyes.*
—JUDGES 21:25

In wrath remember mercy.
—HABAKKUK 3:2

W HAT ON EARTH is going on?
First, COVID-19. It crept into our lives gradually.
In January 2020, I was preaching in Seoul, South Korea.
One or two cases of the coronavirus were reported there.
We flew to London in early February. A few cases of the
virus, said to have come from Wuhan, China, were reported
in the UK. I did not take them seriously. But by early March
things began to change drastically. Life in London became
scary. A high proportion of cases of the virus was in the
very area in which we resided. My physician urged me to
leave England immediately. My preaching schedule for several months had to be canceled.

On March 15, Louise and I flew from Heathrow Airport in London to America. It was the next-to-last plane to leave Heathrow before President Donald Trump stopped all international flights from entering the United States. A lockdown was soon ordered. Reports of COVID-19 showed that cases were rapidly on the rise—now by the thousands. Hundreds of deaths were reported—especially in nursing homes in New York, New Jersey, and Seattle, Washington. People over sixty (both of us are in our eighties) were said to be the most vulnerable. Because hundreds of thousands of people were not allowed to return to work, the national economy was severely affected. Restaurants, schools, and churches were shut down. The increase in unemployment was the highest in living memory. However, by the middle of May things began to improve. People were starting to breathe a sigh of relief.

Secondly, on May 25, 2020, an event took place that may very well live in infamy, like the bombing of Pearl Harbor on December 7, 1941: the evil murder of George Floyd in Minneapolis, Minnesota. A new crisis emerged overnight, promising possibly to create greater fear and concern than that caused by COVID-19. People across the country protested the killing of a Black man by a White police officer. People blamed the police. Thousands all over America were now damaging stores, even ruining many small businesses. Some people demanded abolishing the police altogether, while others called for defunding the police in all cities. A few days after the funeral of George Floyd another White police officer shot and killed a Black man, Rayshard Brooks, in Atlanta. Violence broke out all over again. The chief of police of Atlanta resigned. Renewed calls for the abolishment of police came.

I never dreamed I would see the day that in America there would be vast numbers of people fulfilling Isaiah's warning: people calling evil good and good evil. That is what has been happening before our eyes. The breath of Satan is being felt in nearly every state. Virtually all the news deals with people in the streets protesting with the threat of violence erupting at any moment. None of us has seen anything like this. It is almost as though we had forgotten about COVID-19, although threats of its second wave are now being voiced. The threat of the coronavirus still looms large.

Is God judging America? Is the double whammy best explained as the judgment of God upon us? Yes.

Why would God bother to judge America? Is it because America has a special relationship with Him? Are we like Israel—under a divine covenant?

One thing is certain: as a nation, our forefathers *chose* to bring God into our government. We did not have to call ourselves a nation "under God." We chose to. Consequently, God has honored us. "Blessed is the nation whose God is the LORD" (Ps. 33:12). "Righteousness exalts a nation, but sin is a reproach to any people" (Prov. 14:34).

The difference between God's covenant with Israel and America's relationship with God is simply put: God initiated His covenant with Israel. America chose to be called a nation under God. What is more, without question God has honored America.

But at some stage things began to change. It is difficult to say exactly when. It could have started in very early days. Many of our fathers were slave owners. Did God "overlook" this custom, as Paul once put it? (Acts 17:30). I'm not so

sure. At a personal level there is hardly one of us—meaning
you and me—who would not admit that God overlooked
our foolishness at one time or another but kept on blessing
us. Through the efforts of William Wilberforce (1759–1833),
with the help of hymn writer John Newton (1725–1807),
England declared slavery illegal in 1833. "Amazing Grace"
is probably the best-known hymn in history. In the first
verse Newton says, "Amazing grace, how sweet the sound,
that saved a wretch like me!"[1] Have you any idea what John
Newton was like before his conversion? He wrote his own
obituary to be put on his tombstone. I have taken many
friends to his grave in Olney, Buckinghamshire, England,
to see this firsthand:

> JOHN NEWTON. Clerk. Once an infidel and liber-
> tine, a servant of slaves in Africa, was by the rich
> mercy of our LORD and SAVIOUR JESUS CHRIST
> preserved, restored, pardoned and appointed to
> preach the faith he had long laboured to destroy.[2]

This also shows that England was ahead of America in
dealing with slavery.

Although raised in the Church of the Nazarene, I
became a Southern Baptist. I later went to Southern Baptist
Theological Seminary in Louisville, Kentucky. I took a
course in Baptist history. I was rather shocked to learn that
Southern Baptists had a skeleton in their closet. The opening
comment from my professor, surprising as this may be to
you, the reader, was virtually this: "Embarrassing as it is to
admit, the Southern Baptist Convention was born in 1845
over the slavery issue; it split from Baptists in the North
so that people could own slaves if they wanted to." It is not

unlikely that God's incipient wrath was present even then. And yet it grew to be the largest Protestant denomination in America—14.8 million, 47,456 churches—and was the fastest growing until this slowed down for some reason in the last couple of years.[3]

But when did it become apparent that God did not continue to bless America as He had done for centuries? When America did not win the Vietnam War? The assassination of Dr. Martin Luther King Jr.? When theological liberalism crept into nearly all universities and seminaries? Was it in 1973 when the US Supreme Court passed the *Roe v. Wade* act and approved abortion for any reason without penalty? Was it when same-sex marriage began to accept widespread approval?

I know this: at some stage, an ever-increasing number of Americans began to resent being called a "nation under God" and refuse to recite the Pledge of Allegiance. Some began openly to despise the phrase "in God we trust" on our currency or singing the national anthem.

At the same time, a sense of entitlement has been lurking in the hearts of many American Christians, including evangelicals. We have assumed we are special and that God is obligated to put people in political office who will preserve life as we have known it. In my book *Whatever Happened to the Gospel?* I pointed out that some Christian leaders seem to be more charged up over their right-wing choice of president than they are over spreading the Gospel. They assume that their political choice must be God's choice. It is as though some leaders forget that all men and women are going to die—that they need to be saved—and act as though life in America as we have known it is what must be preserved above anything else.

Is it possible that God is getting us ready for the second coming? If so, this is undoubtedly more important than maintaining life as we have known it. What if the new normal—that nothing will be as it was—is God's way of getting our attention and bringing us to our knees?

FOUR REASONS FOR GOD'S JUDGMENT ON AMERICA

There's a long list of things that have brought about God's judgment on America. Four things stand out in my mind as topping that list. Whether directly or indirectly, each of these connects to our Creator God as written in the Book of Genesis. Genesis teaches that all men and women are created in the image of God. God chose to create all people, male and female. This means that all people in the world—regardless of their skin color—are *human beings for whom Jesus died* (Heb. 2:9; 2 Cor. 5:14–15).

1. Racism

It is written in the Declaration of Independence:

> We hold these truths to be self-evident, that all men are created equal, that they are endowed by their Creator with certain unalienable Rights, that among these are Life, Liberty and the pursuit of Happiness.

The way so many White Americans—including Christians—have treated African Americans for countless years has not gone unnoticed by God. It is not unlike the sin of the early Jerusalem church when middle-class Christians neglected "the poor man" (Jas. 2:6). So today the cries of Black people "have reached the ears of the Lord of hosts" (Jas. 5:4). That is what has happened. God heard these cries and stepped in—to judge us.

In many places Christians have led the way in perpetuating racism. They seem to have forgotten that *all* people are human beings created *equally* in the image of God. They took no notice of this and felt no guilt. I have heard Christian leaders tell racist jokes and laugh their heads off with no apparent pricking of their consciences whatever. Were it not for the sovereign grace of God, I cannot help but wonder why Black people ever embraced the Gospel preached by White Christians. I am not surprised that Black people—from birth to burial to this day—are self-conscious and many are afraid to go out into the public—all because of the color of their skin.

Some Americans hate the notion that black lives matter and despise those leaders who are fighting for justice. Black lives matter to Jesus and, hopefully, to you who read these lines. I doubt it has occurred to many Christian leaders that God has rolled up His sleeves to judge America for the racism that is embedded in our culture. I believe one of the reasons God honored Billy Graham was that he refused to hold a crusade unless all the meetings were entirely integrated. I would also hope that White evangelical leaders—not just the liberals—would lead the way in embracing African Americans.

2. Legalized abortion

This alone demonstrates how America has veered away from God and righteousness. The Bible is clear that life begins at conception. The fact that the six-month-old fetus leaped in Elizabeth's womb when the Virgin Mary showed up with the Son of God in her womb—only a few days old—is infallible proof that John the Baptist and Jesus were human beings then (Luke 1:35–45). Listen to David:

> For you formed my inward parts; you knitted me together in my mother's womb. I praise you, for I am fearfully and wonderfully made. Wonderful are your works; my soul knows it very well. My frame was not hidden from you, when I was being made in secret, intricately woven in the depths of the earth. Your eyes saw my unformed substance; in your book were written, every one of them, the days that were formed for me, when as yet there was none of them.
>
> —PSALM 139:13–16

The Supreme Court's decision in 1973 to allow abortion for any reason without penalty opened the way for countless abortions in the United States. According to the National Right to Life Educational Foundation, well over sixty million abortions have been performed in the United States since 1973.[4] This is incalculably evil. This means over sixty million human beings have been murdered by abortion. That's close to the entire populations of California (39.5 million[5]) and New York (19.5 million[6]) combined! And yet those who uphold millions of abortions call this evil a good thing. The trend is now to embrace the abortion of a child nine months old in the womb! God is angry. The double whammy has descended on us by His judgment. I would not want to be in the shoes of those politicians and supreme court justices who have legalized the murders of these human beings.

3. Contempt for the Creator God

One of the most abused truths in the Bible in recent years is the way people have willfully disregarded God's purpose in making humankind male and female.

> So God created man in his own image, in the image of God he created him; male and female he created them.
>
> —GENESIS 1:27

This was God's idea as to how the earth would be populated. Christian marriage was God's plan and purpose. Sexual intercourse between a man and a woman was not born in Hollywood but at the throne of grace. However, the biblical view of Christian marriage between a man and a woman has been largely eclipsed nowadays by the general approval of same-sex marriage. As recently as ten years ago the majority of Americans disapproved of it. Even President Obama was against same-sex marriage in his first term. His decision to approve of it in his second term led millions to look at it differently and to destigmatize what the Bible regards as an abomination (Lev. 18:20; Rom. 1:26–27). This shows contempt for our Creator God, who with purpose made humankind male and female.

Transgenderism has received much the same public approval as same-sex marriage. People want to claim that they were born in the wrong body and want to change the sex God gave them. While we must unquestionably love and accept those who have undergone procedures to change their sex, I would urge those who are contemplating it not to do it. Statistics show that most who have had this change are sorry, and it does not bring the happiness they expected.

4. Liberalism in churches

Speaking generally, the major denominations have ceased to uphold the divine inspiration of the Holy Scriptures. This is mostly traceable to seminaries and theology departments in universities. This has happened partly because they wanted respectability. They wanted to show that they were on the cutting edge of where theology is going. This is in large part due to taking certain theologians seriously.

The influence of Paul Tillich (1886–1965), Karl Barth (1886–1968), and Rudolf Bultmann (1884–1976) is partly the reason. My theology professor at my seminary said this: "I went from fundamentalism to Barth, from Barth to Tillich, from Tillich to process theology, and now I don't know where I am."

The teaching of open theism, which sadly more and more church leaders are embracing, is essentially process theology: that God is open to us and looks to us for enrichment; He does not know the future but looks to us for input to know what to do. The result has been the absence of a sense of the fear of God. This spread throughout the nation, where there is absolutely no fear of God. The church has ceased to be the "salt of the earth" and have positive influence on government but has generally approved of things such as abortion and same-sex marriage.

It is as though America is now saying, "God, we no longer want You in our nation." Or, as C. S. Lewis (1898–1963) put it:

> There are two kinds of people: those who say to God, "Thy will be done," and those to whom God says, "All right, then, have it your way."[7]

God has responded. He has chosen to judge us. Let us pray that it is not *silent* judgment—the worst possible scenario, as we shall see in the next chapter. I do sometimes fear that America is repeating the era described in the Book of Judges:

> Everyone did what was right in their own eyes.
> —JUDGES 21:25

There were times in ancient Israel when God chose to do nothing but let the nation carry on without Him stepping in.

Chapter Five

IS THERE HOPE FOR AMERICA?

*Let everyone turn from his evil way and from the violence
that is in his hands. Who knows? God may turn and relent
and turn from his fierce anger, so that we may not perish.*
—JONAH 3:8–9

But with you there is forgiveness, that you may be feared.
—PSALM 130:4

*I urge White Christians to take advantage of this special
moment in American history now, to repent of racism and fight
for our Black brothers and sisters in the wake of police
killings. I believe if we miss this moment, we would have failed
in our generation....Most of us White people are simply out of
sight and out of mind; we are oblivious to [what Black people
experience and feel]. We cannot let this moment pass. White
people have not asked enough about the experience of Black
people. I can only imagine the indignity, the
emotional indignity. I can only imagine it. White people need
to fight for racial justice and go through a period of contrition.*
—DAN CATHY, CEO, CHICK-FIL-A

WHAT HAS WORRIED me most as I have written this book is that many well-meaning White Christians will hastily dismiss any need to sympathize with Black people.

Ask this question: How do you suppose Jesus would feel? If He could have compassion on a multitude "because they were harassed and helpless, like sheep without a shepherd," how much more would He understand how people feel

when they are quickly dismissed because of their skin color
or because they have not had the education, the care, the
love and acceptance most White people have utterly taken
for granted?

"Every person is worth understanding," said Clyde
Narramore (1916–2015).[1] I am pretty sure we would lower
our voices and climb down from our lofty pedestals of comfort and pointing the finger if we knew all that was know-
able about people we hastily dismiss. The question is, Do
we want to know more about them?

I now turn to the subject of chastening, or disciplining,
following the pattern of the writer of the letter to the
Hebrews. As soon as he urges us to focus on "looking into
Jesus," who is seated at the right hand of the throne of God,
he asks a question:

> Have you forgotten the exhortation that addresses
> you as sons? "My son, do not regard lightly the dis-
> cipline of the Lord, nor be weary when reproved
> by him. For the Lord disciplines the one he loves,
> and chastises every son whom he receives."
> —Hebrews 12:5–6

Going back to the Old Testament verse that inspired this
book's title, Joshua was preparing people to come into their
inheritance. They had never been that way before. But first
they would need to learn to expect what preceded coming
into their inheritance. Similarly, the writer of Hebrews
was helping his readers understand what they were going
through—as part of their preparation. Strange as it may
seem, they were undergoing chastening.

Could this be the explanation for what you are going through now?

It is so easy to forget this. The doctrine of chastening is often neglected when it comes to Christian teaching. And yet it is so comforting when we realize that God's disciplining us is the explanation of what could be going on in our lives.

I will never forget how I discovered the doctrine of chastening. It was on an August afternoon in 1956. My father virtually rejected me over my new theological understanding. My grandmother had given me a new 1955 Chevrolet when I began pastoring a church in Palmer, Tennessee, but took it back when she could see I would not remain in my old denomination. I was distraught—not so much from handing back the car as from the sense of God deserting me. I honestly thought my dad and grandmother would be thrilled with my new teaching. In prayer that day I cried out to God, "Why?" when unexpectedly "Hebrews 12:6" entered my mind. I had no idea what that verse was. So I turned to it in my little King James New Testament. It read:

> Whom the Lord loveth he chasteneth and scourgeth every son whom he receiveth.

This was a new concept for me, but instantly I could see that what was going on in my life those days was God at work in a different kind of way. I was immediately able to see that it was a vital part of my preparation for the future. I could not think of anything I had done that was sinful. Yet I knew God was allowing my family—and many friends— to reject me as part of His preparation for me. It opened up a new world of thought. I went on to explore this teaching in ever-increasing measure. It became integral to my theological understanding generally and the premise interwoven throughout many of the books I have written, beginning with my first book, *Jonah*.

Has it crossed your mind that God might be chastening *you*? Could it be that God is trying to get your attention? You may say, "God already has my attention." But is it possible that He wants more from you than you have presumed? I have personally thought a thousand times that God truly has my attention—only to discover by His grace that He did not have my attention, as I had thought. It is like being asleep; you don't know you were asleep until you wake up!

God's chastening is essentially preparation. It is not God getting even with us; He got even at the cross. The blood of Jesus satisfied the justice and wrath of God. This is why David could say, "As far as the east is from the west, so far does he remove our transgressions from us" (Ps. 103:12). The word *paideuei* in Hebrews 12—chastens, disciplines—means enforced learning. It is when God teaches us a lesson. He can be very strict like a relentless schoolteacher who does what it takes to secure the needed change in us. But God carries this out entirely because He loves us. Indeed, He chastens only those He loves. If we were not disciplined, it would show we are "illegitimate children and not sons" (Heb. 12:8). We should therefore rejoice when we are chastened; it is a sign we are truly saved.

THREE KINDS OF CHASTENING

There are three kinds of chastening: internal, external, and terminal.

1. Internal chastening

This is God's plan A. It's when God speaks to our hearts through His word. This can be painful. It operates on us. Sometimes God does not use an anesthetic. It cuts. It hurts. After all, the Word of God is "living and active, sharper than any two-edged sword, piercing to the division of soul and of spirit, of joints and of marrow, and discerning the thoughts and intentions of the heart" (Heb. 4:12).

As painful as it might be, God dealing with us through His word is the best way to have our problems solved. If God speaks to you through His word—even though you see its demands could cost you a lot, take it! Take it with both hands. It will save you incalculable regret down the road. So when God speaks to you through His word, my advice to you is to say, "Yes, Lord"—then and there.

2. External chastening

This is plan B. God turns to this when plan A does not achieve the change in us that He wanted. God spoke His word to Jonah (plan A): "Go to Nineveh, that great city, and call out against it" (Jon. 1:2). God said, "Go," and Jonah said, "No." If only Jonah had listened to God's word—the call that went right to his heart. But he did not heed the word. And God turned to plan B. Because "Jonah rose to flee to Tarshish" (Jon. 1:3) and got on a ship going there, "the LORD hurled a great wind upon the sea, and there was a mighty tempest on the sea" (Jon. 1:4). Plan B began to work when Jonah was in the belly of a fish: "Then Jonah prayed" (Jon. 2:1).

More often than not, God uses plan B to get our attention because we have not sufficiently prayed. What will it take for you to pray? God wants your time. He loves your company. Will it take being swallowed up by the equivalent of a big fish to get you to pray? What we know is it worked with Jonah: "*Then* Jonah prayed." Not only that; God secured the response in Jonah He was after. Enforced learning worked. After the fish ejected Jonah and God repeated His original order to go to Nineveh, "Jonah arose and went to Nineveh" (Jon. 3:3). Plan B worked.

3. Terminal chastening

What if plan B had failed? Answer: plan C—terminal chastening—would be put into effect. Pray that God does not resort to this in your case. Terminal chastening means death. It is the "sin that leads to death" (1 John 5:16).

Christians in Corinth had abused the Lord's Supper. Paul answered a question they must have asked: Why are people in our church ill, weak, sickly, and some have died? Having pointed out how they had abused the Lord's Supper (1 Cor. 11:20–29), he then answers, "This is why many of you are weak and ill [plan B], and some have died [plan C]" (v. 30).

The generation of Israel that did not make it to the Promised Land were those with whom God was not pleased (1 Cor. 10:5). God swore in His wrath that they would not enter His rest (Heb. 3:11). They died in the wilderness, being an example of terminal chastening.

This also goes to show that God *expects* us to ask *why* when extraordinarily bad things happen—such as the coronavirus and the violence we have been seeing in America.

So is our double whammy God's judgment on the United States of America? Yes.

FIVE KINDS OF JUDGMENT

That said, there are five kinds of judgment of God: retributive judgment, gracious judgment, redemptive judgment, natural judgment, and silent judgment.

Which of these is God's judgment on America? First, let me define each of these.

1. Retributive judgment

This is when God gets even. It is when His full wrath is poured out. God warned Adam not to eat of a particular tree in the Garden of Eden. Otherwise he would bring death upon himself (Gen. 2:16–17). Adam disobeyed. "The wages of sin is death" (Rom. 6:23). We read later in Genesis: "All the days that Adam lived were 930 years, and he died" (Gen. 5:5). This is retributive judgment. *Retributive* means deserved and severe punishment, not to improve a person but to mete out punishment for its own sake. It is like the Mosaic law that requires "eye for an eye, tooth for a tooth" (Exod. 21:24). The biblical teaching of eternal punishment is retributive judgment. It is not for correcting, improving, or changing a person; it is punishment for sin.

2. Gracious judgment

This is *partly* retributive and *partly* merciful—but it is *always* a warning. Retributive judgment is the wrath of God poured out in "full strength" (Rev. 14:10). The King James Version renders this as "the wrath of God without mixture." By contrast, gracious judgment is mixed with mercy. Jesus said, "Those whom I love, I reprove and discipline" (Rev. 3:19). Therefore, where there is gracious judgment, painful though it is, there is also hope. This type of judgment *can be partly* retributive—to the point of plagues coming. But why? Answer: to induce repentance. When He is angry, God may send judgment, yes. But He is doing it to warn us, to stop us. He may send a plague to turn us around.

This is what happened with Jonah. You will recall that when God told Jonah to go to Nineveh, Jonah said no and ran from God. So God sent a great fish, and it swallowed Jonah. It was judgment, but it was mostly a warning. As we saw previously, God secured the response He wanted in Jonah. Therefore, at the bottom of it all was gracious judgment.

Are you running from God?

3. Redemptive judgment

This is partly retribution and partly promise. This can be seen on the occasion when the children of Israel murmured against God. God sent poisonous snakes that bit the people. People were dying all over the place. But God ordered Moses to make a fiery serpent and set it up on a pole, and all who were bitten and looked upon the serpent would live (Num. 21:8). Moses held up the serpent of brass, and all who looked on it lived. This then is redemptive judgment. It is a variation of gracious judgment.

4. Natural judgment

This is a variation of retributive judgment, with the emphasis being on the inevitable consequences of sin. It is a principle that may be summed up in the saying "You reap what you sow." There is a natural judgment at work. It could be explained simply as the consequence of sin. It is a natural law at work.

5. Silent judgment

This is when God appears to do nothing. This is, to me, in a sense, the scariest judgment of all. If I have learned anything from a study of Romans 1:18–32, it is that when God is angriest, He does *nothing*. God never loses His temper like you and I do. We may think that if God gets really mad, He is going to show it immediately. But God isn't like that. "The wrath of man worketh not the righteousness of God" (Jas. 1:20, KJV). We may think we can tempt God. We may think we can needle Him. Or challenge Him to send a bolt of lightning. But the angrier God is, the calmer He is, because time is on His side. He can wait. He has an awful lot of patience.

When Pontius Pilate sent Jesus to Herod, Herod was glad to see Him. He hoped that Jesus might perform a miracle before his eyes. So Herod questioned Jesus at some length, but Jesus "made no answer" (Luke 23:9). Utter silence. Since Jesus said He only did what He saw the Father doing (John 5:19), we know that this mirrored the Father's response to Herod.

In a word, when God is at His angriest, He doesn't do anything. He doesn't send pain. He doesn't even send a warning. There is no hint that God sent a warning to Sodom and Gomorrah. Suddenly, without warning to its inhabitants, God sent fire and brimstone (Gen. 19). When sin and promiscuity prosper, God may choose to be silent. Those who have defied God go right on in their evil deeds. And you say, "Dear Lord, how can You let people do that?" Remember that David also raised this issue:

> Fret not yourself because of evildoers; be not
> envious of wrongdoers! For they will soon fade
> like the grass and wither like the green herb.
> —PSALM 37:1–2

Yes, that "soon" may seem like an eternity to us, and we wonder why God doesn't do something! Billy Graham once wrote that his wife, Ruth, after reading part of a book he was writing that described the downward spiral of America's morals, surprised him by saying, "If God doesn't punish America, He'll have to apologize to Sodom and Gomorrah."[2]

America is under God's judgment *right now.*

Good news. It is *gracious judgment.* There is hope. Yes. Millions of Christians are praying. God is not being silent. To quote Cardinal Dolan again, "He is right in the middle of it."

There were no believers that we know of in Sodom and Gomorrah except Lot's family. It would seem that only Abraham knew that judgment was coming to Sodom and Gomorrah. This is when he made a statement with a question that all of us need to embrace:

> Shall not the Judge of all the earth do what is just?
> —GENESIS 18:25

This is the attitude we should take when the double whammy of COVID-19 and the civil unrest caused by racial tension is upon us. Believe it or not, strange as it may seem, God is at work.

America is under judgment—yes. But thankfully it is not God's silent judgment. It is His gracious judgment. Millions of Christians should be encouraged. It is one of the ways by which He drives us to our knees. We should pray for mercy that God will grant grace by which we may see His glory.

Our *only* hope: another great awakening. The people of Nineveh repented, and God sent great revival.

God can do it again, and I believe He will.

But He wants us to know His ways.

Chapter Six

LEARNING GOD'S WAYS

When your children ask their fathers in times to come, "What
do these stones mean?" then you shall let your children
know, "Israel passed over this Jordan on dry ground." For
the LORD your God dried up the waters of the Jordan for you
until you passed over, as the LORD your God did to the Red
Sea, which he dried up for us until we passed over, so that all
the peoples of the earth may know that the hand of the LORD
is mighty, that you may fear the LORD your God forever.
—JOSHUA 4:21–24

Gratitude is one of the greatest Christian
virtues; ingratitude, one of the most vicious sins.
—BILLY GRAHAM (1918–2018)

O NE OF THE things uppermost on Joshua's mind was
that he wanted those who would enter the Promised
Land to know God's ways. God said of the previous generation of the children of Israel—those who died in the wilderness and whom God swore in wrath would not enter His
rest—"They have not known my ways" (Heb. 3:10).

To be very candid, I fear deeply for the present generation
of Christians. I have been preaching for sixty-six years—
since 1954. We spent twenty-five years in London, and in
my old age, since 2002, I have been privileged to travel all
over the world and all over America. That does not mean I
have been everywhere, nor does it mean this qualifies me to
be an expert in diagnosing the present situation. But if I am
totally honest, and if I am true to myself, I have an uneasy

feeling that most people who are in church are frighteningly shallow and do not know God's ways. I thank God for the exceptions. But I fear that most pastors do not have a deep prayer life, neither do they know their Bibles very well. As for sound teaching, one cannot help but think it is deemed unimportant. Preaching nowadays is mostly motivational—aimed at making people "feel good" rather than teaching the Bible. "Seeker-friendly churches" have taken their toll, resulting in superficiality. Singing worship songs is given more time than preaching in many places—sometimes it is twice as long, and the theological content in both, I fear, is about one inch deep.

Here we are in the greatest crisis imaginable. Are we prepared for this?

I have an even greater fear that we have not learned our lesson. All we seem to care about is "getting back to normal" so we can return to watching baseball games on Saturdays and pro football games on Sundays. The truth is, as I have said, the new normal is that nothing will likely be normal again. We have forgotten that we are all going to die one day and that all men and women will face judgment when they die (Heb. 9:27). Our crises should remind us that this life is not all there is; there is coming for all of us an eternity.

What is more, life at its longest is still short. You will undoubtedly think this when you are dying, when *your time has come*. Not only that, dear reader; eternity lasts a long time.

Is God getting your attention?

There is no doubt that God is judging America. He loves

us. It is because people are going to hell and God wants them to go to heaven.

The early Methodists learned their theology from their hymns. Most of them are God-centered. So many songs sung in church today are the opposite of God-centeredness. It is one of the curses of the "me generation." We ask, "What's in it for me?" and it hardly crosses our minds to ask, "What's in it for God?"

God wants us to know His ways.

Bobby Conner says it like this: "We have become too casual with a holy God we barely know." Bobby has noted pastors who come to the pulpit wearing flip-flops and wearing Bermuda shorts. On the other hand, some dress nicely and genuinely attempt to extol the majesty and sovereignty of God, but their doctrine of the Trinity is "God the Father, God the Son, and God the holy Bible." I'm sorry, but many don't seem to have a clue what the immediate and direct witness of the Spirit is. Dr. Martyn Lloyd-Jones used to say of some of them: "perfectly orthodox, perfectly useless."

THREE THINGS GOD WANTS TO TEACH US

There are three things Joshua wanted to teach those children of Israel who were about to enter Canaan: gratitude, expectancy, and the awe of God.

1. Gratitude

Joshua required that a man from each tribe of Israel pick up a stone from the exact area on the bed of the river Jordan where the children crossed on dry ground and then put these stones in a heap. This would cause future Israelites to ask, "What do these stones mean?" These people would grow up being reminded that it was the exact spot where their fathers crossed the Jordan on dry land.

What was the purpose of this? To teach them gratitude. Joshua was afraid that they would forget. We are all like that. We think we will remember, we promise to remember, but we forget. God has a way of teaching us not to forget things that matter.

This was the reason for keeping the Passover. God gave specific instructions to Israel from the very night of the Passover that this was a memorial to keep forever. "This day shall be for you a memorial day, and you shall keep it as a feast to the LORD, throughout your generations, as a statute forever, you shall keep it as a feast" (Exod. 12:14).

This was the reason Jesus instituted the Lord's Supper, or Communion: to teach us gratitude. It was to remind us of the most important day in the history of the world—when Jesus died on the cross for our sins. The bread and wine remind us that Jesus had a physical body and that His blood was shed for the forgiveness of our sins (Matt. 26:28). It is called the *Eucharist*, which means giving of thanks. We partake of the bread and wine because we are remembering to be thankful. "Do this in remembrance of me" (Luke 22:19). Thus we have Passover in the Old Testament and Holy Communion in the New Testament. Both rituals have in common the recognition of blood. "When I see the blood, I will pass over you" (Exod. 12:13). "This cup...is the new covenant in my blood" (Luke 22:20).

Consequently, the setting up of the stones from the bed of the river Jordan was to be a "memorial forever" (Josh. 4:7). Joshua wanted to teach them God's ways, that they would know what pleases God and what displeases Him. Our showing gratitude is a priority with God, and you and I must *remember* to make it a priority in our lives.

I would lovingly say to you, my reader, that if you and I expect to cope and have joy and pcacc through these difficult days, we must show deference for God's ways. God has His ways just as you have your ways. I have my ways. People may not like your ways. You may not like God's ways. But He is the only God you've got! If it is the God of the Bible, the Father of Jesus, and the God who sends the Holy Spirit that you want to be your God, you must adjust to Him. He won't conform to you and me. Furthermore, He won't bend the rules for any of us!

God notices when we are thankful and when we are not. Jesus healed ten lepers. Only one leper came back to Him to say thank you. Jesus' immediate reply was to ask what happened to the other nine who got healed but did not show gratitude (Luke 17:17).

Here are three principles you can be sure of: (1) God loves gratitude, (2) God hates ingratitude, and (3) gratitude must be taught. And that is precisely what Joshua was doing.

I want also to list three pragmatic reasons for showing gratitude. First, it could make a huge difference in whether your prayer is answered. "In everything by prayer and supplication, *with thanksgiving*, let your requests be made known to God" (Phil. 4:6). *Always* remember to be thankful when you pray. Second, several years ago, Mayo Clinic said in its monthly bulletin (which I receive) that researchers had clinically proved that thankful people live longer. It makes a difference in your health. Third, you will know beyond doubt that you please God. Which gives you more satisfaction, when God is pleasing you, or when you are pleasing God? My suggestion: learn to get your satisfaction from knowing you please God rather than demanding that He pleases you by giving things you enjoy.

Let me make one more suggestion before I move on. Every night before you go to bed, name at least three things that happened *that very day* for which you are thankful to God. I promise you, it is one of the best habits you will ever develop.

2. Expectancy

Charles H. Spurgeon is often quoted as saying, "You might not always get what you want, but you always get what you expect."[1] Expectancy can make a huge difference in whether we live in perpetual fear or maintain a real confidence in these troublesome times. We've never been this way before, and we must keep our eyes steadfastly on the Lord Jesus Christ. Headlines in newspapers and television news have often reported that COVID-19 has taken a toll on Americans' mental health. Cases of suicides, nervous breakdowns, and excessive drinking at unprecedented levels are being reported in many places, mostly owing to lockdown for many weeks. Having expectancy that we will make it through these perilous times will keep one with a level head. People simply want to know that they will make it through this crisis—that they will have a job, that they will be financially secure, and that they won't get terminally ill or see their loved ones die.

There are three levels of expectancy. The first is the *natural level*. One should not underestimate this. God made us the way we are. Some people are born optimists. I knew a man like this. He was so much fun to have around. People like this sometimes weather a storm better than those who are always negative and looking at the dark side of things. Is God more likely to find an entry point by which one's morale is boosted in people like this? Possibly. God's "common grace"—referring mainly to the way He made us and shaped us—could be the way some people live in the expectancy that "something good is going to happen to me today."

That said, I hope you will aspire to reach for a higher level of expectancy than what is natural.

The second level is *trusting wholly in the word of God.* Certain Puritans called it "the indirect witness of the Spirit." The Holy Spirit is mediated by the word. It is the Holy Spirit bearing witness with our spirit (Rom. 8:16). This wonderful method of getting to know God's ways builds up your faith. This is what we all need as we cope with the double whammy we are going through. You can rely on this statement as you discover its reliability for yourself:

> Those who trust Him wholly find Him wholly true.
> —FRANCES R. HAVERGAL (1836–1879)[2]

This is what God wants of you. It is what pleases Him. This is what I mean by getting your satisfaction by what pleases Him rather than being happy only when He does things that please you.

> Without faith it is impossible to please him, for whoever would draw near to God must believe that he exists and that he rewards those who seek him.
> —HEBREWS 11:6

How does God reward those who lean on His word? A thousand ways. He will never leave you nor forsake you (Heb. 13:5). He has a way of giving you tokens of His presence in a way you know you are not being deceived. It is what will keep you going "from strength to strength" (Ps. 84:7), from "glory to glory" (2 Cor. 3:18, KJV)—that is, from "one degree of glory to another."

> The love of Jesus, what it is
> None but His loved ones know.
> —BERNARD OF CLAIRVAUX (1090–1153)[3]

The third level is *oath level assurance*. Next to seeing Jesus face to face when we get to heaven, this is the highest level of getting to know God's ways. It is the immediate and direct witness of the Holy Spirit. The Greek word is *plerophoria*—full assurance.

This was the way Joshua led the children of Israel. Notice carefully how it is put: "*When* your children ask..., 'What do these stones mean?'" (Josh. 4:21). Joshua shows he does not have the slightest doubt that the waters of the Jordan will "cut off from flowing, and the waters coming down from above shall stand in one heap" (Josh. 3:13). *This had not happened yet!* And yet Joshua is so sure that it will happen that he tells all the people what to say when future generations ask, "What do these stones mean?"

In other words, Joshua had faith that it was as though it already happened!

That is the expectancy Joshua demonstrated to all the children of Israel. They do not proceed toward the Jordan asking, "What if this does not happen?" Joshua does not approach the Jordan and suddenly panic and say to himself,

"Oh dear, what if the waters of the Jordan don't roll back?" How could Joshua have such faith?

It was the same when Elijah told King Ahab that it would not rain until he said it would!

> As the LORD, the God of Israel, lives, before whom
> I stand, there shall be neither dew nor rain these
> years, except by my word.
>
> —1 KINGS 17:1

How could Elijah be so sure? If he saw a cloud, did he bite his nails and say, "Oh dear, what if it starts raining? I could never show my face in Israel again. My prophetic reputation will be ruined."

The answer is, God had sworn an oath to him. Elijah uses oath language: "As the LORD...lives." He wasn't worried for a second.

But only one who has had God swear an oath to him or her can have that kind of confidence.

That is how Joshua knew. He assured the children of Israel that the waters of the Jordan would stand up and they would cross on dry land as they had crossed the Red Sea under Moses. By speaking as he did, he engendered confidence in these people who were keeping their eyes on the ark of the covenant.

They were getting to know God's ways. That means that God has power to give us assurance like that too. We should pray for it. Jesus talked about a faith that was so strong that one should ask but simultaneously believe he has already received it (Mark 11:24). In the same way, John speaks of knowing we will receive what we "have asked of him" (1 John 5:15).

Dr. Martyn Lloyd-Jones was my predecessor at Westminster Chapel. He told me that during the years when Hitler bombed London in World War II, in 1941–42—when the buildings around the chapel were being destroyed right, left, and center—God witnessed to him that the bombing would not touch the chapel. And it didn't.

I don't say this level of expectancy happens all the time. But it can happen. And does happen. And when we know that this kind of expectancy is possible, we all should fall on our knees in earnest prayer and ask God to do this for us during this time of concern.

3. Knowing the awe of God

This is borne out by Joshua's continued instruction to the children of Israel. God will be performing the miracle of crossing the Jordan on dry land "that you may *fear* the LORD your God forever" (Josh. 4:24, emphasis added). One of the ways of God is that He wants us to fear Him—not to be afraid or scared to death but to respect Him in utter awe.

There are two ways by which you and I might come to know this fear of the Lord. The first is when you experience it for yourself. For example, when something happens before your eyes—like an extraordinary miracle—it may well give you a sense of awe. This is what Joshua meant; the Israelites would discover how *real* God is. Such a sense of awe is not a secondhand report of something that happened to someone else. It is one thing to hear of an incident that caused people to have a sense of awe, but it is totally different when you experience this firsthand. Joshua wanted them to learn the fear of the Lord by what they experienced.

It would increase their faith for what they would be required to do many times later as they come into their inheritance.

I grew up in a church in Ashland, Kentucky, in which I experienced the fear of God directly many times. It had a direct effect on my personal life. I have thought that we may have been at the tail end of the influence of the Cane Ridge Revival (1801), which was a hundred miles away. My first pastor was Gene Phillips. There was an anointing on his preaching that caused me to fear. John Newton referred to the fear of God in the second verse of his hymn "Amazing Grace":

> 'Twas grace that taught my heart to fear,
> And grace my fears relieved;
> How precious did that grace appear
> The hour I first believed![4]

Jacob endured a brief era of backsliding, but when he returned to Bethel and repented, he then persuaded his children to put away all their idols. The result was that "terror from God fell upon the cities" wherever Jacob and family traveled (Gen. 35:1–5). When Jesus performed miracles, the result often was the people were "filled with awe" (Luke 5:26). Part of the outcome of the Holy Spirit falling at Pentecost was that "awe came upon every soul." The Greek word is *phobos*, which means fear. This happened after the Holy Spirit struck Ananias and Sapphira dead (Acts 5:11).

At the height of the Great Awakening in New England, Jonathan Edwards' sermon "Sinners in the Hands of an Angry God" (1741) resulted in such awe that people held on to church pews and embraced trees to keep from falling into hell. In the Cane Ridge Revival, called America's

Second Great Awakening, a sermon on the Judgment Seat of Christ, based on 2 Corinthians 5:10, produced so much awe that hundreds fell to the ground spontaneously. There were never fewer than five hundred people flat out on the ground over a period of four days.

Have you ever experienced the fear of the Lord first-hand? A man with an experience is never at the mercy of a man with an argument.

That said, there is a second way to come to know the fear of God. It can be taught. David said,

> Come, O children, listen to me; I will teach you
> the fear of the Lord.
>
> —Psalm 34:11

This does not mean that you work up a sense of awe. No. It means an utter respect for God's ways and His word. It is what leads to wisdom. "The fear of the Lord is the beginning of wisdom" (Prov. 9:10). The fear of the Lord will lead you to respect God's commands.

For example, have you ever wondered why the Book of Proverbs has so much to say about sex and adultery? Take, for example, the in-your-face warnings against adultery (Prov. 5–7). It is because sexual promiscuity and wisdom won't mix. Sexual purity leads to wisdom. Those who foolishly disobey God's commands regarding sexual purity end up doing foolish things. They lack wisdom.

In my earlier list of reasons I believe God is judging America, I did not mention sexual promiscuity in the church. One reason is that those who indulge in it often get caught and find themselves openly judged anyway. However, I know more than I wish I did regarding sexual promiscuity in the church—including some of the best-known evangelical churches and Charismatic churches. Too many pastors turn a blind eye to what they know is going on in their congregations. They don't want to lose members and consequently say little or nothing. The result is twofold: (1) an absence of the fear of God and (2) the absence of wisdom. This is apart from the hundreds and hundreds of ministers that lose their ministry from sexual indiscretion.

As we saw previously, an aspect of the glory of God is God's opinion. That is what wisdom is. It is knowing the next step forward, knowing what to do. It is having twenty-twenty foresight vision. We all have twenty-twenty hindsight vision. "If only I had not said that. If only I had not done that." True wisdom will save you so much regret. The anointing will teach you all you need to know (1 John 2:27). Remember, it does not come from education or a high IQ. It begins with the fear of the Lord.

Therefore, one can be *taught* not only to keep God's commands but equally to be *scared to disobey* God lest His chastening descend upon you, as we saw regarding the church at Corinth. The fear of God's discipline should be enough to keep all of us out of trouble!

"My people are destroyed for lack of knowledge" (Hos. 4:6). This includes the knowledge of God's ways.

As you and I endure the current double whammy storm—and any storms we face beyond it—we need to know God's ways. Some people know *about* God. But knowing *about* God will not enable us to come out of these crises triumphant. We need to know God Himself.

This comes by knowing His ways.

Chapter Seven

HEAVEN—OR HEAVEN ON EARTH?

And the people passed over opposite Jericho. Now the
priests bearing the ark of the covenant of the LORD stood
firmly on dry ground in the midst of the Jordan, and all
Israel was passing over on dry ground until all the nation
finished passing over the Jordan....And the LORD said to
Joshua, "Command the priests bearing the ark of the testi-
mony to come up out of the Jordan." So Joshua commanded
the priests, "Come up out of the Jordan." And when the priests
bearing the ark of the covenant of the LORD came up from
the midst of the Jordan, and the soles of the priests' feet were
lifted up on dry ground, the waters of the Jordan returned
to their place and overflowed all its banks, as before.
—JOSHUA 3:16–17; 4:15–18

If you read history you will find that the Christians that did the
most for the present world are just the ones that thought the
most of the next. The Apostles themselves, who set on foot, in
the conversion of the Roman Empire, the great men who built up
the Middle Ages, the English Evangelicals who
abolished the Slave Trade, all left their mark on Earth,
precisely because their minds were occupied with Heaven. It is
since Christians have largely ceased to think of the
other world that they have become so
ineffective in this. Aim at Heaven and you get the
earth "thrown in:" aim at earth and you'll get neither.
—C. S. LEWIS (1898–1963)

THERE ARE BASICALLY two opinions among Christians
as to how we should apply the crossing of the Jordan

to our lives. For example, many hymns and songs refer to the crossing of the Jordan as death and Canaan as heaven. The closing verse in the famous hymn "Guide Me, O Thou Great Jehovah" says:

> When I tread the verge of Jordan,
> Bid my anxious fears subside
> Bear me through the swelling current,
> Land me safe on Canaan's side:
> Song of praises,
> I will ever give to Thee.
>
> —WILLIAM WILLIAMS (1717–1791)[1]

Johnny Cash (1932–2003) recorded a song about not having to cross the Jordan alone. It's one I heard many times as I grew up. And yet in my old Nazarene church we used to sing the following song all the time. It refers not to death but rather to experiencing entering Canaan, which was interpreted as a second work of grace—entire sanctification:

> Why wander in the wilderness, O fainting soul,
> Come over into Canaan land;
> By faith cross over Jordan tho' the waves may
>   roll,
> Come over into Canaan land.
>
> Come over into Canaan land,
> Come over into Canaan land,
> Where the grapes of Eschol grow,
> Where the milk and honey flow,
> Come over into Canaan land.
>
> —HALDOR LILLENAS (1885–1959)[2]

Charles Wesley's popular hymn "Love Divine, All Love
Excelling," when originally written referred to the "second
rest" in verse 2:

> Breathe, O breathe thy loving Spirit,
> Into every troubled breast;
> Let us all in thee inherit,
> Let us find that second rest.
> —CHARLES WESLEY (1707–1788)[3]

The "second rest" actually referred to a second work of
grace as his brother John Wesley (1703–1791) taught (and
Nazarenes followed). John Wesley taught that the "rest" in
Hebrews 4:9 (KJV)—"There remaineth therefore a rest to
the people of God"—was a second experience following
conversion. This was his understanding of the "rest" in
Hebrews 4:1–10, which is based upon the children of Israel
entering Canaan. The writer of Hebrews refers to entering
Canaan as entering into rest. God swore in His wrath that
the children of Israel who wandered in the desert forty years
would not enter into His rest, namely Canaan. Most hym-
nals change Charles Wesley's words and make it "promised
rest."

In other words, there are at least two interpretations
regarding crossing the Jordan: (1) dying and going to heaven,
and (2) entering into victorious living. Some would call the
latter "heaven on earth." Taking the latter view does not in
any case tie one to Wesley's teaching of sanctification.

The main argument against the view that crossing the
Jordan refers to death is that the children of Israel crossed
the Jordan to fight countless battles. Surely we will not fight
battles in heaven! I do not know how crossing the Jordan

was first interpreted as dying and going to heaven. But it probably became the predominant way crossing the Jordan was understood, at least in many songs and hymns.

In this chapter we continue to follow the pilgrimage of the ancient children of Israel. These Israelites were going where they had never been. What they did we too must do. What they experienced we can experience.

In a word, they became a part of a real miracle, crossing the Jordan on dry land as the waters were kept from flowing until they all crossed it. They were privileged to see God repeat a miracle, namely like the children of Israel who crossed the Red Sea on dry land. Sometimes God is pleased to repeat what has been done before; sometimes He never repeats something that has happened before. The manna would shortly come to an end and never be repeated. The pillar of cloud by day and fire by night would never be repeated. But God graciously let the new generation see what their forefathers had seen.

What you and I can learn from their crossing the Jordan is this: we need to see for ourselves *how real God is*. Again, God may repeat Himself, but usually He does not. As I said before, those described in Hebrews 11 had in common that no person of faith got to duplicate what had been done before. They focused their eyes on heaven. This is what we learn about Abraham. What kept him going was that "he was looking forward to the city that has foundations, whose designer and builder is God" (Heb. 11:10). Indeed,

> These all died in faith, not having received the
> things promised, but having seen them and greeted
> them from afar, and having acknowledged that

> they were strangers and exiles on earth. For people
> who speak thus make it clear that they are seeking
> a homeland. If they had been thinking of that land
> from which they had gone out, they would have
> had opportunity to return. But as it is, they desire
> a better country, that is, a heavenly one. Therefore
> God is not ashamed to be called their God, for he
> has prepared for them a city.
>
> —HEBREWS 11:13–16

What kept motivating all these people of faith, then, was this: they knew that this present life is not all there is. They had their eyes on heaven. Indeed, the writer of Hebrews gives yet another exhortation: "For here we have no lasting city, but we seek the city that is to come" (Heb. 13:14). And yet, lo and behold, they accomplished amazing things on earth! All these people of faith did extraordinary things. It goes to show what C. S. Lewis said: people who have their eyes on heaven accomplish the most on earth, because those who aim at heaven get the earth "thrown in," but those who aim at the earth "get neither."

TWO THINGS GOD WANTS TO ACCOMPLISH

I believe God has allowed the double whammy in America at present to get our attention. I believe He wants to accomplish two things in us:

1. To let us experience for ourselves how real, wonderful, true, faithful, and glorious God is. It could be spectacular—like the children of Israel crossing the river Jordan—or something less dramatic but just as real—as when God spoke

to Elijah with "the sound of a low whisper" (1
Kings 19:12; "still small voice" in KJV).

2. To remind us that we are going to heaven. That
   is our destination. This life is not all there is. We
   are not existentialists—having to live these days
   as though there is no purpose in life. The God of
   the Bible is a God of purpose. And to the degree
   we focus on His Son, who died on the cross so
   that we might go to heaven, we will accomplish
   more on earth than we ever dreamed.

We all need to discover sooner or later whether what we
believe is true. Real. Valid. Pure gold.

Consider Jacob. He was not a very nice man. He was
a liar and a cheat. Certainly very, very unworthy to be in
the heritage of his father and grandfather. He would grow
up hearing about his legendary grandfather, Abraham. How
would you like to grow up hearing about the accomplish-
ments of those in your family or church before you came
along? You would feel inferior. Incapable. But at one of
Jacob's lowest moments—when he was running away from
home because of the injury he had done to his brother
Esau—Jacob came to "a certain place." He had no idea
that it was holy ground. He took a stone for a pillow as he
retired for the night.

And he dreamed, and behold, there was a ladder
set up on the earth, and the top of it reached to
heaven. And behold, the angels of God were
ascending and descending on it! And behold, the
LORD stood above it and said, "I am the LORD,
the God of Abraham your father and the God of

Isaac.... Behold, I am with you and will keep you wherever you go, and will bring you back to this land. For I will not leave you until I have done what I promised you."

—GENESIS 28:12–15

When Jacob woke up from his sleep, he said, "Surely the LORD is in this place, and I did not know it" (v. 16).

What happened was this: Jacob needed to experience for himself how real God is. He could not have imagined that there would be a cliché that would be repeated billions of times over the next centuries: "The God of Abraham, the God of Isaac, and the God of Jacob."

God wants to do this for you. Perhaps God has never been that real to you. But He wants to bring you to a place whereby you can say it honestly but with glory in your soul: "I've never been this way before."

One more thing: whether it be a spectacular miracle or something unspectacular, it is not up to us to make something happen. We don't have to "work it up" or "imagine" something to happen that is not happening; our task is to focus on the ark of the covenant—fulfilled in the Lord Jesus Christ—and watch God do the work. Focus on Jesus.

Chapter Eight

THE REPROACH

Today I have rolled away the reproach of Egypt from you.
—JOSHUA 5:9

Truth is generally the best vindication against slander.
—ABRAHAM LINCOLN (1809–1865)

D O YOU KNOW what it is like to be unvindicated? This means that your reputation is under a cloud. You would love to have your name cleared, that both your friends and enemies would see you as having been falsely accused or misunderstood.

This chapter is for you.

There was more that the children of Israel would need to do before they crossed the Jordan on dry land. All the men needed to be circumcised—that is, those men who were born since they left Egypt forty years before (Josh. 5:5). It was a sign of the covenant, going back to Abraham (Gen. 17:9–11). Joshua wanted to make sure all male Israelites had been circumcised. It showed that they were unashamedly the children of Israel, that they were the people of God.

An unexpected bonus came to the children of Israel during this time. "Today I have rolled away the reproach of Egypt from you" (Josh. 5:9).

The word *reproach* means shame. It means to bear a stigma; to be discredited, dishonored, or disgraced. It refers to the way you are perceived or how you think you are perceived. It is embarrassing because it punctures your pride.

When Rachel, who had been barren, finally bore a son to Jacob, she said, "God has taken away my reproach" (Gen. 30:23). Barrenness had a long tradition of referring to shame. The prophet Isaiah could exclaim, "Sing, O barren one, who did not bear....Fear not, for you will not be ashamed; be not confounded, for you will not be disgraced" (Isa. 54:1, 4).

This chapter is important mainly for this reason: Christians today, speaking generally, are not very respected. They are often laughed at, mocked, put down, seen as mostly ignorant, and not held in high esteem. This is in contrast to the way Christians in the earliest church were regarded: "None" of the unbelievers "dare join them [Christians], but the people held them in high esteem" (Acts 5:13).

I believe that the double whammy we are in will end up changing all this. God did not allow this crisis for nothing; I believe it will lead to America's third Great Awakening, eclipsing the New England Awakening and the Cane Ridge Revival. It is what I have elsewhere referred to as the Word and Spirit coming together.

TWO KINDS OF REPROACH

The word *reproach* is to be applied two ways: (1) a reproach that God does not want us to have. An example is what Joshua called "the reproach of Egypt" that God removed from the children of Israel just before they went into Canaan. The reproach removed was like an open vindication for them—even before the walls of Jericho fell. However, there is (2) a reproach that God does want us to have and that we gladly bear for the glory of Christ. Peter and John rejoiced—it was as though (if I may be forgiven for putting it this way) they could not believe their luck—that they were counted "worthy" of bearing the *shame of the name* of Jesus (Acts 5:41). They were thrilled with this reproach. This came about by a measure of vindication "by the Spirit," that which Jesus fully experienced (1 Tim. 3:16). I shall return to this.

What was "the reproach of Egypt"? It was a stigma of at least four things on the Israelites.

1. It was a sense of shame that had been attached to them all the way from Egypt, where they were a nation of slaves. Who would respect slaves?

2. It referred to the taunts and reproaches that were leveled at them by the Egyptians. They were mocked because they wandered in the desert all those forty years and were not able to go into the land of Canaan (Num. 14:16).

3. They were regarded as a sort of Egyptian (Num. 22:5). Their being circumcised now demonstrated they were truly Israelites, not only upholding the Abrahamic covenant but identifying with the fact that Moses had been circumcised, this being the way Pharaoh's daughter knew that the baby Moses was a Hebrew (Exod. 2:6).

4. The first three points show what would have affected the way the Israelites had seen themselves. Those who died in the wilderness would have been demoralized until the day they died. It was a generation of people who had nothing to live for—only to die in the desert because they did not follow Joshua and Caleb when they could have entered Canaan forty years before (Num. 14:30–33). God had sworn in His wrath they

would not enter His rest (Heb. 3:10). They didn't.
Their dismay would have rubbed off on those men
who were younger and now required to be circumcised. Joshua assured them that they were a
new generation; they would indeed be crossing the
Jordan. Joshua announced, "Today I have rolled
away the reproach of Egypt from you" (Josh. 5:9).

They did not need to feel identified with the previous
generation; they were today's men. The reproach they had
borne until the day they were circumcised, then, was not a
stigma God wanted them to have. As long as they bore that
kind of reproach, nobody would be afraid of them. Who
would be scared of slaves? Who would be frightened of
Egyptians? Who would be afraid of people who had wandered in the desert for all those years but could not enter
Canaan? Nobody feared those people in the wilderness!
They were weaklings, pitiful.

But that changed overnight. When they crossed the
Jordan on dry land, word spread like wildfire all over
Canaan.

> As soon as all the kings of the Amorites who were
> beyond the Jordan to the west, and all the kings of
> the Canaanites who were by the sea, heard that the
> LORD had dried up the waters of the Jordan for the
> people of Israel until they had crossed over, their
> hearts melted and there was no longer any spirit in
> them because of the people of Israel.
>
> —JOSHUA 5:1

When the Israelites learned that their enemies' hearts
"melted," it was like an open vindication. They now had

tremendous confidence. They knew they were not slaves.
They were not Egyptians. No longer would people taunt
them and say they were losers.

It can be so encouraging when your enemy is afraid of
you. This is what gave Gideon courage. He overheard a man
telling a dream to his comrade.

> "Behold, I dreamed a dream, and behold, a cake
> of barley bread tumbled into the camp of Midian
> and came to the tent and struck it so that it fell
> and turned it upside down, so that the tent lay flat."
> And his comrade answered, "This is no other than
> the sword of Gideon the son of Joash, a man of
> Israel; God has given into his hand Midian and all
> the camp."
>
> As soon as Gideon heard the telling of the
> dream and its interpretation, he worshiped. And he
> returned to the camp of Israel and said, "Arise, for
> the LORD has given the host of Midian into your
> hand."
>
> —JUDGES 7:13–15

THE CHRISTIAN INFERIORITY COMPLEX

I believe that many in the church today have an inferiority
complex. We know we are not respected. It hurts. No one
fears God; no one fears the church. The world thumbs their
noses at us, and we look like helpless infants.

We are like the children of Israel *before* the "reproach of
Egypt" was rolled away from them.

We need to be reminded that our enemy, the devil, is resist-
ible: "Resist the devil, and he will flee from you" (Jas. 4:7);
"Your adversary the devil prowls around like a roaring lion,

seeking someone to devour. Resist him, firm in your faith" (1 Pet. 5:8–9). The purpose of the roar of a lion is to scare off. The effect of a satanic attack is often to scare us and make us think we are defeated when we are not, to make us think we have given in when we haven't. As John said, "He who is in you is greater than he who is in the world" (1 John 4:4).

A part of the "reproach of Egypt" is the way we perceive ourselves. It is also traceable to the way we are perceived. We know how the world laughs and does not respect us. Part of this is that we are ashamed of the kind of reproach we *should* embrace, as I will explain later.

We must resist listening to the mocking of the world; it is the same as listening to the devil. Don't believe the devil. The devil is a liar (John 8:44). And yet, as William Perkins (1558–1602) put it, "Don't believe the devil, even when he tells the truth!" The devil will not only quote Scripture but also point to what the world says about us. The purpose is to intimidate us and demoralize us.

God does not want us to have the reproach of Egypt, but there is a reproach that He *does* want us to have, namely bearing the stigma for the glory of Christ's name. This is a reproach that we should welcome. It is an internal vindication, vindication by the Spirit. Jesus was "vindicated by the Spirit" (1 Tim. 3:16). It was an internal vindication; it is what He had in His heart—the total approval of the Father. It was noted at His baptism: "This is my beloved Son, with whom I am well pleased" (Matt. 3:17). It was manifested again when He was transfigured before the disciples: "This is my beloved Son, with whom I am well pleased; listen to him" (Matt. 17:5).

Jesus never was vindicated externally. The Pharisees

did not believe in Him. The five thousand who followed him after He fed them with the loaves and fish dwindled to the twelve (John 6:66–67). Herod did not vindicate him. Neither did Pilate. The Jews demanded His crucifixion. His vindication came from the Father by the Spirit.

Even after He was resurrected, there was no external vindication. Did he go to Herod's or Pilate's house on Easter morning and say, "Surprise!"? Certainly not. He could have, but His vindication would continue to be internal—that is, what is revealed by the Holy Spirit.

To this very day He is still being vindicated by the Spirit. It continued at Pentecost when three thousand were converted. This was by the Spirit. When you and I were converted, it was the work of the Holy Spirit (John 6:44). We did not see Him face to face. His external vindication will come one day when, after His second coming, "at the name of Jesus every knee should bow, in heaven and on earth and under the earth, and every tongue confess that Jesus Christ is Lord, to the glory of God the Father" (Phil. 2:10–11).

In the meantime, you and I must get our vindication as Jesus did. Although He was given the Spirit "without measure" (John 3:34), you and I have a "measure of faith" (Rom. 12:3). We must not look to people for approval. We get our vindication internally—as Jesus did. It is by the Spirit that we are enabled to seek only the approval of God (John 5:44).

That means we will let our critics pick us to pieces. We let them call us fools. They will say things that make us look stupid. The essence of the stigma is a feeling of being embarrassed. And yet if we truly—truly—embrace the reproach for the name of Christ, we will be like Peter and

John. They *rejoiced* over the inestimable privilege of suffering "dishonor for the name" (Acts 5:41).

How can we do this? How can we be so sure? Answer: because we know we have the *truth*.

After all, truth is the best vindication against slander.

Chapter Nine

THE MANNA

And the day after the Passover, on that very day…the
manna ceased the day after they ate of the produce of the
land. And there was no longer manna for the people of Israel,
but they ate of the fruit of the land of Canaan that year.
—JOSHUA 5:11–12

I'm on a seafood diet; I see food, I eat it.
—DOLLY PARTON

GOD KNOWS WE have to eat to stay alive. I have often
thought how interesting it is that Jesus put the petition
"Give us this day our daily bread" before He gave us the spiritual petitions in the Lord's Prayer. (See Matthew 6:11–13.)
It is not easy to think about spiritual things with an empty
stomach. William Booth (1829–1912), the founder of the Salvation Army, often said that it is hard to preach the Gospel to
people with an empty stomach[1]. So he fed them first.

Most of us have not worried too much about having
enough food in our supermarkets. We usually get what we
need. If what we want is not there, we complain to the store
manager. We expect food to be on the shelves.

I always took the availability of food for granted—that is,
until I visited food stores in Poland and Russia before the
Berlin Wall was torn down on November 9, 1989. It was a
shock to me. We visited a supermarket in Warsaw, and the
shelves were almost empty throughout the store. There was
no meat, no bread.

I was equally shocked when Louise and I visited our local

supermarket immediately after we returned from London on March 15, 2020. The coronavirus crisis was the cause of so many shelves being empty for several days; everybody had rushed to the store and hoarded food and supplies as though we were going to have nothing for a long while—especially toilet paper. It reminded me of stores in the old Soviet Union. I kept asking, "Is this America?"

In addition to stores being short on certain supplies due to increased demand, many restaurants closed, and when they reopened, it was for curbside pickup or delivery only. So the COVID-19 lockdown changed many of our eating habits—at least temporarily in most places. Many could certainly say, "We've never been this way before."

I don't think there were any overweight people in the wilderness during the forty years the children of Israel wandered there. God supplied them with what they needed to survive. At the beginning of those forty years the people began to complain that there was no food. They grumbled and said to Moses and Aaron:

> Would that we had died by the hand of the LORD in the land of Egypt, when we sat by the meat pots and ate bread to the full, for you have brought us out into this wilderness to kill this whole assembly with hunger.
>
> —EXODUS 16:3

At that time, God graciously stepped in and gave them supernatural food called manna. First, the "glory of the LORD appeared in the cloud" (v. 10) as they looked toward the wilderness. Second, the next morning "dew lay around the camp" (v. 13).

> And when the dew had gone up, there was on the
> face of the wilderness a fine, flake-like thing, fine as
> frost on the ground. When the people of Israel saw it,
> they said to one another, "What is it?" For they did
> not know what it was. And Moses said to them, "It
> is the bread that the LORD has given you to eat."
>
> —EXODUS 16:14–15

Manna means "What is it?" They called this food manna.
"It was like coriander seed, white, and the taste of it was
like wafers made with honey" (Exod. 16:31), also like "the
taste of cakes baked with oil" (Num. 11:8). God told them
to eat as much as they wanted. It was supernatural food.
No matter how much they gathered to eat—even if it was a
lot—there was none left over. Those who gathered little had
no lack. They could bake it or boil it. If they left part of it
until the morning, it "bred worms and stank" (Exod. 16:20).
They were given just enough for each day; God supplied
what they needed.

The day before Sabbath, however, they were supposed
to save it so there was enough to eat on the Sabbath. The
manna did not come on the Sabbath.

> The people of Israel ate the manna for forty years, till
> they came to a habitable land. They ate the manna
> till they came to the border of the land of Canaan.
>
> —EXODUS 16:35

Sure enough, following the circumcision, having kept
the Passover (Josh. 5:10), the manna ceased. I have long
been amazed at this.

> And the day after the Passover, on that very day, they ate of the produce of the land.... And there was no longer manna for the people of Israel, but they ate of the fruit of the land of Canaan that year.
>
> —Joshua 5:11–12

Ten Takeaways From the Miracle of Manna

We are to learn some lessons from the era of the manna in the wilderness.

1. God provided food supernaturally when there was no natural food in the wilderness. It is a reminder that God takes care of us at the natural level.

2. This food was provided for a disobedient generation. They were the same people God swore in His wrath would not enter His rest—that is, into the Promised Land of Canaan (Heb. 3:11). Unworthy though they were, God looked after them. After all, they were His people who had kept the Passover and crossed the Red Sea on dry land.

3. The people got tired of the manna. "Oh that we had meat to eat! We remember the fish we ate in Egypt that cost nothing, the cucumbers, the melons, the leeks, the onions, the garlic. But now...there is nothing at all but this manna to look at" (Num. 11:4–6). It gives us a hint that though we pray for God to show up supernaturally, we might get so used to it that we take it for granted and cease to appreciate it.

4. God's typical plan for us is to eat natural, physical food from the land. The manna was for a

special era—one that is not likely to be repeated.
God gave them manna for all those years, but
it stopped on the "very day" it was no longer
needed.

5. God knows exactly what we need—food, shelter,
clothing; He promised to supply our need. Our
duty is to seek first the kingdom of God and His
righteousness, and the rest will be added to that
(Matt. 6:33).

6. Whether God shows up supernaturally or natu-
rally, we should be equally grateful for the way
He chooses to supply our need.

7. We must not overestimate the importance of the
supernatural and suppose it alone reveals God's
glory; His glory can be as present in the natural
as it is in the supernatural.

8. It is the healthy Christian who can recognize any
way God may choose to look after us—whether
supernatural healing or the use of medicine and
physicians. Paul could perform miracles and pray
for physical healing (Acts 28:8) and yet instruct
Timothy to take "a little wine for the sake of your
stomach and your frequent ailments" (1 Tim. 5:23).

9. On the "very day" the manna stopped, the children of Israel ate "unleavened cakes and parched
grain" (Josh. 5:11). Could it be they all were tired
of the manna? Why did God stop the manna?

10. All supernatural eras come to an end. All
revivals come to an end. All trials come to an

end. God wants us to live by faith no matter
what the situation is that He provides.

Jonathan Edwards taught us that the task of every generation is to discover in which direction the sovereign
Redeemer is moving, then move in that direction. The only
way we can do this is by keeping our eyes on Jesus Christ.
He will show us the next step forward in our journey here
as we continue to go where we've never been.

Chapter Ten

THE PASSOVER

While the people of Israel encamped at Gilgal [the area where
circumcisions took place], they kept the Passover on the four-
teenth day of the month in the evening on the plains of Jericho.
—JOSHUA 5:10

Let us honor the blood of Jesus Christ every moment
of our lives, and we will be sweet in our souls.
—WILLIAM J. SEYMOUR (1870–1922)

T HE PASSOVER WAS God's protection of the children of
Israel when the tenth plague struck Egypt and King
Pharaoh. Moses warned Pharaoh with plague after plague
that Pharaoh must set them free. Pharaoh kept refusing,
having a hard heart that would not give in. Then came the
ultimate plague on Egypt. God told Moses and Aaron to
take a one-year-old lamb and sprinkle its blood on each side
of the doorposts and lintel of the houses. They would eat
the lamb roasted in fire.

> You shall eat it in haste. It is the LORD's Passover.
> For I will pass through the land of Egypt that
> night, and I will strike all the firstborn in the land
> of Egypt, both man and beast; and on all the gods
> of Egypt I will execute judgments: I am the LORD.
> The blood will be a sign for you, on the houses
> where you are. And when I see the blood, I will

pass over you, and no plague will befall you to
destroy you, when I strike the land of Egypt.

—EXODUS 12:11–13

God destroyed all the firstborn in Egypt as the angel of
God passed all over Egypt. This included Pharaoh's own
firstborn. At long last Pharaoh gave in and let the people go.
The Israelites ended up passing through the Red Sea on dry
land. Finally, Israel was free.

The Passover would be a memorial to be kept forever.
God wanted to be sure that Israel would always be grateful
and never forget that night of nights. What is paramount in
the Passover is God's focus on the blood. "When I see the
blood, I will pass over you" (v. 13).

HONOR THE BLOOD

I was named after my father's favorite preacher, Dr. R. T.
Williams. Dr. Williams gave this word of instruction to
preachers: "Honor the blood, and honor the Holy Ghost."
This word has not ceased to grip me. I pray daily—many
times—for the blood of Jesus by the Holy Spirit to be sprinkled on me. I pray for the sprinkling of the blood of Jesus
upon the minds of those listening when I preach. I begin
every day and end every evening praying for the sprinkling
of the blood of Jesus. I started each chapter of this book
praying for the blood to be sprinkled on me as I wrote.

When Moses inaugurated God's covenant with Israel, he
"took the blood [that had been put in a basin] and threw
it [most versions say 'sprinkled'] on the people and said,
'Behold the blood of the covenant that the LORD has made
with you" (Exod. 24:8).

The writer of Hebrews refers to the fact that in prayer we come "to Jesus, the mediator of a new covenant, and to the sprinkled blood" (Heb. 12:24), which refers to Jesus' blood that was sprinkled on the heavenly mercy seat. Peter begins his first letter referring to "God the Father, in the sanctification of the Spirit, for obedience to Jesus Christ *and for sprinkling with his blood*" (1 Pet. 1:2). These three things—sanctification, obedience, and sprinkling of blood—are all present moments and ongoing privileges and benefits in our relationship with God.

The same is assumed in 1 John 1:7. The blood is applied as we walk in the light. Walking in the light brings us "fellowship with one another, and the blood of Jesus his Son cleanses us from all sin." All these verses refer to the ongoing privileges and responsibilities in our relationship with God. These are not past-tense experiences that refer merely to a once-for-all conversion; they are all referring to present-tense privileges and responsibilities.

When God prepared the children of Israel in Egypt for the Passover, He made it clear this would be remembered annually.

> This day shall be for you a memorial day, and you shall keep it as a feast to the LORD; throughout your generations, as a statute forever, you shall keep it as a feast.
>
> —EXODUS 12:14

There was no Passover feast—which includes eating a lamb—during the forty years in the desert; their only food was the manna. But as soon as they could—right after the time of circumcision—they kept the Passover. Never forget

the meaning of the words *pass over*: "When I see the blood,
I will pass over you" (v. 13).

Passover honors the blood. It points to its ultimate fulfill-
ment thirteen hundred years later. The blood sprinkled on
each side of the doorpost and over the doorpost is a clear
prophetic preview of Jesus hanging on the cross.

> See, from his head, his hands, his feet,
> Sorrow and love flow mingled down.
> Did e'er such love and sorrow meet,
> Or thorns compose so rich a crown?
> —ISAAC WATTS (1674–1748)[1]

The children kept the Passover just before crossing the
Jordan for these reasons: (1) as obedience to God, who stip-
ulated that Passover was to be kept as an annual feast, (2)
to show gratitude to God for the way He looked after them
for the forty years, and (3) they wanted to honor God just
before they entered Canaan.

As we continue to cope with where we've never been
before, let us be faithful to honor the blood. Doing this is
extolling the cross, honoring Him who died and bringing
glory to God, who sent His Son to die for us. It is the safest
and most God-centered way to live through what is coming
ahead.

Chapter Eleven

HOLY GROUND

When Joshua was by Jericho, he lifted up his eyes and
looked, and behold, a man was standing before him with
his drawn sword in his hand. And Joshua went to him and
said to him, "Are you for us, or for our adversaries?" And
he said, "No; but I am the commander of the army of the
LORD. Now I have come." And Joshua fell on his face to the
earth and worshiped and said to him, "What does my lord
say to his servant?" And the commander of the LORD's army
said to Joshua, "Take off your sandals from your feet, for the
place where you are standing is holy." And Joshua did so.
—JOSHUA 5:13–15

Tread softly! All the earth is holy ground.
—CHRISTINA ROSSETTI (1830–1894)

ONE OF MY early mentors was Dr. N. Burnett Magruder
(1914–2005). A graduate of Yale, he was the man
chiefly responsible for introducing me to the writings of
Jonathan Edwards. I once suggested to Dr. Magruder back
in August 1956 that surely the highest level of devotion to
God would be to die as a martyr for the Lord. He smiled,
took out a small piece of paper, and wrote a brief sentence,
which I have carried with me for years: "My willingness to
forsake any claim upon God is the only evidence that I have
seen the Divine glory." It is perhaps the profoundest statement I have come across outside the Bible. I still ponder
it. It touches on the depth—the bottomless pit—of our
self-centeredness.

I sometimes think that examining the human heart is somewhat like peeling the layers of an onion. As Jeremiah put it, "The heart is deceitful above all things, and desperately sick; who can understand it?" (Jer. 17:9). I could not have guessed back in 1956 that there would be those who uphold a view that God needs us and exists only to bless us and make us feel good; therefore, we can demand Him to do things for us. According to Dr. Magruder, seeing God's glory is to affirm Him, even if He does not make us feel good, and grant Him the right to be Himself without us. As Job put it, "Though he slay me, I will hope in him" (Job 13:15). The closer we get to God, the more He requires that we respect His sovereignty.

That is precisely what was happening with Joshua and this man with the drawn sword. Joshua had more to learn about God's ways. Moses had tutored him for many years. He was present at the Passover and experienced the crossing of the Red Sea. He witnessed the pillar of cloud by day and the pillar of fire by night. He was one of the spies who went into Canaan and agreed with Caleb that the children of Israel should immediately go into the land. He was utterly faithful and loyal to Moses. He saw the serpent of brass that Moses lifted before the people when they had sinned so deeply. He lived on the manna in the desert like everybody else. God chose him to succeed Moses, who then laid his hands upon Joshua. God assured Joshua that He would be with him just as He had been with Moses (Josh. 1:5).

But Joshua now faced a new and different challenge. He saw a remarkable figure, a man with a drawn sword. Joshua recognized this man's power and authority. Joshua knew immediately that this stunning figure was a force to be reckoned with; he did not want this man to be on the enemy's side—that is for sure. Joshua's worst fear was that this man might be on the side of the very people that the children of Israel had a mandate to conquer.

After hearing Joshua's question, "Are you for us, or for our adversaries?" the man's reply is strange: "No." Joshua's question did not require a yes-or-no response, but the man said, "No." Many translations say "Neither."

What kind of an answer is that? Whether "no" or "neither," it was not very helpful or encouraging. Joshua thought that if God were with him, as He had been with Moses, surely such a stunning figure would be with him and the children of Israel.

But the man continued, "I am the commander of the army of the LORD. Now I have come."

FOUR DISCOVERIES FROM JOSHUA'S ENCOUNTER

Joshua was to discover four things through his encounter with the awesome man with the drawn sword. These discoveries teach us about the holy ground of God's sovereignty. Let's explore them now.

1. The man was utterly on God's side and concerned only about God's will.

If the man is truly on God's side, does not that mean he is necessarily on our side? No. The man with the drawn sword took instructions from God alone. God exists for His own glory. The God of Joshua is the polar opposite of the "What's in it for me?" generation in America today. Joshua might have thought along those lines and wondered, "What's in it for us?" But the answer was, nothing except the joy and thrill of seeing God give countless victories without anybody on earth getting the credit—only God.

Joshua was being taught to get his satisfaction from seeing God glorified—that is, God getting all the credit. This made Joshua see that he was not entitled to demand anything from God. He had no "claim" on God; he could not say, "God, You owe me something." The awesome man with the drawn sword served notice on Joshua that he was not on either side—only on the Lord's side. Joshua needed to learn that God wants to be worshipped when we concede that He is not obligated to us. We are totally dependent on His mercy. We forsake any claim upon God but worship Him for being *God*. It is a matter of enjoying God being God without any reference to us.

Joshua was being taught to see the glory of God differently. He could have said that he had seen the glory merely because he saw the pillar of cloud by day and fire by night. I think that some of us want to see only visibly so that we can say we saw God's glory. God can certainly do this, yes. But Joshua saw God's glory by faith—hearing the word from the commander. It was an aspect of the glory that went beyond anything he had conceived up to now; it was nothing visible. It referred to God's sovereignty, His doing whatever He pleased, as the psalmist put it (Ps. 115:3). Joshua therefore needed to learn that he had no claim upon God. He could never put God on the spot and force Him to do anything. Seeing the glory in this way therefore refers to affirming God to be Himself without Him having anything to do with us or for us.

2. The man was an angel.

Angels are God's "ministering spirits, sent out to serve for the sake of those who are to inherit salvation" (Heb. 1:14). Angels have infinite power that is derived from the infinite God. They are devoted to the will of God. They cannot be bribed. They resent anyone trying to worship them. In a word: angels are perfect worshippers of God.

3. Joshua was put in his place.

Whereas he assumed that *he* was the commander of the children of Israel, Joshua now discovers he has been completely outranked. It was not Joshua who was in charge; it was this angel. Joshua was now learning that this man with the drawn sword was the *true* commander of the Lord's armies. This man will do the leading, the instructing, the advising, and be the military genius that orchestrates all victories. Joshua will not be able to get any credit for successes in Canaan.

4. An army Joshua did not know existed—a host of unseen angels—would defeat the enemy.

In other words, it would not merely be the trained men of Israel who would bring victory but God's angels. There is no doubt that at the human level the men of Israel—now circumcised and devoid of the reproach of Egypt—were trained and fit. Indeed, forty thousand were ready for war (Josh. 4:13). But it would be the armies of the Lord in the heavens—like ten thousand drones that no one can see—who will make miracles happen. This was the only explanation for the parting of the river Jordan. As it would be put in Elisha's day years later: "those who are with us are more than those who are with them [the enemy]" (2 Kings 6:16).

Joshua then asked the commander if he had any further word for him. The angel replied, "Take off your sandals from your feet, for the place where you are standing is holy" (Josh. 5:15).

Joshua was not conscious that he was on holy ground. He needed to be taught that. Moses was not aware that he was on holy ground when he saw the burning bush. He needed to be taught.

What makes a bit of ground holy? It is when and where God shows up. He can do this anywhere at any time. This means that the most insignificant place can be declared holy when God moves in. It can come when you least expect it.

This means that all the earth is holy.

> The earth is the LORD's and the fullness thereof, the world and those who dwell therein, for he has founded it upon the seas and established it upon the rivers.
>
> —PSALM 24:1–2

> Holy holy, holy is the LORD of hosts; the whole earth is full of his glory!
>
> —ISAIAH 6:3

At the burning bush, Moses had to take off his shoes because he tried to figure out what God did not want him to figure out. Joshua took off his shoes when he learned that he did not have to fight his battles; this is what God would do.

WHAT DOES THIS TELL US?

What can we learn from Joshua's having to take off his shoes? First, it is a small thing for God to send another great awakening. The armies of heaven will defeat the powers of darkness.

Second, whereas God could dispatch angels without our being around, He has chosen to *use those who are equipped*. Paul said to Timothy, "Do your best to present yourself to God as one approved, a worker who has no need to be ashamed, rightly handling the word of truth" (2 Tim. 2:15).

Third, sometimes God does nothing except in answer to prayer. Strange as it may seem, those who labor on earth in praying nonstop get God's attention in heaven.

Could it be that you are called to a ministry of prayer? Perhaps you have little or no profile or you are not the most educated person around. Maybe you have no great talent to speak, to write, or to sing. Perhaps you feel you have no gifts of the Spirit. Interestingly, there is no "gift of prayer" in 1 Corinthians 12:8–10 or Romans 12:3–8. But you can pray.

> Satan trembles when he sees
> The weakest saint upon his knees.
> —WILLIAM COWPER (1731–1800)[1]

These things said, the next great move of God will result in our affirming Him for who He is and what He is like rather than a God whom we can play with as if He were a toy, a God nobody respects. We need an outpouring of the Holy Spirit that will cause people to fall at Jesus' feet "as though dead" (Rev. 1:17). That was the effect that the Lord of glory had on John on the Isle of Patmos.

And yet when we are used—and are successful—who gets the glory? We are fools if we fancy that success lies with us. As the psalmist put it,

> Not to us, O LORD, not to us, but to your name give glory.
>
> —PSALM 115:1

We do not need to be afraid of the present or the future. We do not need to be scared because we are traveling where we've never been. The commander of the Lord's army will fight for us. He will be there just when we need Him—never too early, never too late, but always right on time.

Chapter Twelve

THE NEXT GREAT AWAKENING

And the LORD said to Joshua, "See, I have given Jericho
into your hand, with its king and mighty men of valor."
—JOSHUA 6:2

Have you no wish for others to be saved? Then
you are not saved yourself, be sure of that!
—C. H. SPURGEON

I BELIEVE THAT THE double whammy crisis we are now in will lead to the next great move of God on the earth. This will come about not because brilliant men will by their intellect convince atheists of the existence of God. Nor will it come because legislation will help quiet civil unrest. It will come not because vaccines put an end to the coronavirus crisis.

The next great move of God will come when ordinary people by the hundreds are convinced that people need to be saved—that the Gospel is the only hope—and are unafraid and unashamed to say this to anyone.

I wish it were not true, but the only apparent result of the double whammy at the moment is fear. Great fear. Fear of illness. Fear of dying. Fear of violence. Fear of economic downturn. Fear of change.

I'm sorry, but America has not learned her lesson yet.

Paul said to Timothy, "God gave us a spirit not of fear but of power and love and self-control" (2 Tim. 1:7). John said, "There is no fear in love, but perfect love casts out fear" (1 John 4:18). These two statements are either true, or they are not. Because they are true, there will be those who are unashamed of the Gospel and will be filled with love for people, no matter their race or political views; they will have a genuine love for the Gospel and whoever needs to be saved. Such people are a vital part of the key to bring about the next great awakening.

THE MOST DANGEROUS PEOPLE ON EARTH

You will recall that the people of faith in Hebrews 11 did great things on earth because they had their eyes on heaven. It will likewise be people today who have their eyes on heaven and are unafraid to die who will do the greatest good on earth and who will be leading the way in seeing people saved during the next great move of God. My friend Josif Tson used to say to me, "The most dangerous person in the world is one who is unafraid to die."

Are you afraid to die? Are you dangerous because you are a threat to Satan? Are we like those people who thought casting out demons was a fun game—that is, until a demon leaped on them after saying, "Jesus I know, and Paul I recognize, but who are you?" (Acts 19:15). The demon in hell (Gr. *tartarus*) knew about Jesus; they knew about Paul. But most of us are not known in hell because we are no threat to Satan's interests. I want to be known in hell; I would prefer to be more famous there than on earth.

God is not looking for people whose aim is to effect political change. He is not looking for those who merely want to return to their comfortable lifestyles. He is looking for those who are willing to go outside their comfort zones and obey God.

There is to be found in the account of Joshua conquering Jericho a picture—a blueprint—of the only kind of Gospel that will bring a great awakening. It is a Gospel that gives God all the glory, just as Joshua learned that it would be the army of the Lord that would do the real fighting. Joshua would get no glory. Indeed, it is interesting that Joshua's name is not even mentioned in Hebrews 11. God mentioned Abel, Enoch, Noah, Abraham, Sarah, Isaac, Jacob, Joseph, and Moses. But when it came to the conquering of Jericho, it says: "By faith the walls of Jericho fell down after they had been encircled for seven days" (Heb. 11:30). It does not say whose faith! Remember, "There is no limit to what a man can do or where he can go if he does not mind who gets the credit." Joshua knew in advance that the walls of Jericho would fall and that it would be God who did it.

KEYS TO THE NEXT GREAT MOVE OF GOD

When God said to Joshua, "See, I have given Jericho into your hand," Jericho was still shut tight inside and outside (Josh. 6:1–2). There are three things we may learn from this. First, the Lord was assuring Joshua *in advance* that the battle was already won. God knows the future perfectly. As St. Augustine (354–430) said, "A God who does not know the future is not God." When the Apostle Paul was ready to go to the next assignment, God told him in a vision to stay put—right where he was in Corinth: "I have many people in this city who are my people" (Acts 18:10). God called them "my people" before they were converted! Likewise, God said that Jericho was conquered before Joshua conquered it. After all, God knows the future and therefore knows who will be saved. God knows the end from the beginning (Isa. 46:10). Not only that; God told Paul not to be afraid.

> Go on speaking and do not be silent, for I am with
> you…for I have many in this city who are my
> people.
>
> —ACTS 18:9–10

Paul stayed. The result was the founding of a great church in Corinth, and Paul's two letters to the Corinthians in our New Testament followed.

Second, this is showing us the essence of the Gospel—that righteousness is imputed to us by faith alone apart from works. If God saved us by our works, the glory would go to us. But God saves us by grace through faith (Eph. 2:8). He honored Abraham's faith. When Abraham was an old man and had no heirs, God told him to count the stars; "so shall your offspring be." Abraham might have said to God, "Stop joking with me; do you expect me to believe something as impossible as that?" But no. Abraham believed God's word, and God "counted" Abraham's faith as "righteousness" (Gen. 15:6). Righteousness was imputed to Abraham but also to all who believe the Gospel (Rom. 4:5). Paul used this account as exhibit A in his unfolding of justification by faith alone in Romans chapter 4.

I have noted elsewhere in some of my books that the key to the next great move of God would be the Book of Romans and especially Romans chapter 4, which is all about Abraham's faith. This is what God used in previous awakenings on both sides of the Atlantic. The first Great Awakening began largely from Jonathan Edwards weekly preaching justification by faith from 1733–1738 in Northampton, Massachusetts. Martin Luther came to see that faith alone—that is, faith by itself—satisfies the passive justice of God. It led to the great Reformation in the sixteenth century and the world being turned upside down. It was John Wesley hearing someone read from Luther's preface to his commentary on Romans in a Bible study on Aldersgate Street in London May 24, 1738, that led to his heart being "strangely warmed." The eventual result was the great revival in England in the eighteenth century, with him and George Whitefield (1714–1770) leading the way. It was parallel to the Great Awakening in America.

This kind of teaching and preaching is desperately needed today. There are millions of Americans like the Pharaoh who knew nothing about Joseph (Exod. 1:8)— who show contempt for our heritage and want to tear down statues and burn the American flag. There are likewise tens of thousands in the church who know little or nothing about Romans and Romans chapter 4. Instead of standing for the Word of God, there are now those who are claiming boldly, "There is a new breed of prophets arising that will not only know the future but cause it." Wrong! Things cannot get much worse than that. Such a breed will encourage you to believe them rather than Scripture. There are sadly those who don't read their Bibles because they look for a "prophetic word" all the time. Their folly will be manifest soon. It is like living on cotton candy.

There is a third thing implied by Jericho being shut tight; it is a picture of two things.

- First, it is a picture of the spiritual condition of *all* people. We are all born "dead in trespasses and sins" (Eph. 2:1). Only the Holy Spirit can give life; no one can come to Christ unless he or she be drawn by the Holy Spirit (John 6:44).

- Second, it is a picture of America. There is no fear of God in the land and little if any in the church, speaking generally. Seeing hundreds of thousands of Americans turning to God in weeping for their sins would be the equivalent to the walls of Jericho falling spontaneously.

We must face it. A massive turning to God is our only hope. A vaccine may or may not come along, which will abate the deaths of people with COVID-19. There is more hope, humanly speaking, for Americans being spared physically than there is for our spiritual healing. This is because only God by a sovereign intervention of the Holy Spirit can save America.

Only God could conquer Jericho. Only God can save.

The children of Israel were required to do something very odd:

> You must march around the city, all men of war going around the city once. Thus shall you do for six days. Seven priests shall bear seven trumpets of rams' horns before the ark. On the seventh day you shall march around the city seven times, and the priests shall blow the trumpets. And when they make a long blast with the ram's horn, when you hear the sound of the trumpet, then all the people shall shout with a great shout, and the wall of the city will fall down flat, and the people shall go up, everyone straight before him.
>
> —Joshua 6:3–5

Why ever would God require these people to do such a thing? God could have commanded Joshua to do everything the first hour of the first day; there is nothing impossible with Him (Jer. 32:17; Luke 1:37). God's ways are higher than our ways and His thoughts higher than our thoughts (Isa. 55:8–9). He could have caused the wall of Jericho to fall without the first person marching around the city. But one of His ways is that He often asks us to do things that make no sense—like asking Abraham to give up Isaac when Isaac was the promised child (Gen. 22:2).

Why is it that sometimes God waits for us to pray? Here is probably the most quoted and most repeated conditional promise in the Old Testament:

> If my people who are called by my name humble themselves, and pray and seek my face and turn from their wicked ways, then I will hear from heaven and will forgive their sin and heal their land.
>
> —2 Chronicles 7:14

Many are doing this. Are you doing this? Many more need to be praying like this—humbling themselves and turning from their sins—and not give up. We must never *ever* give up.

The children of Israel marching around the city for seven days is not only analogous to praying; it is an example of doing something that shows we believe God's Word and are unashamed to do what we are told to do. It is bearing a stigma. It means to be embarrassed. I would have thought that the most embarrassing thing on earth is to believe the Bible and to share the Gospel with another person.

- The children of Israel could have felt like fools walking around the city once a day for six days and then seven times on the seventh day.

- Naaman the leper must have felt like a fool when he was told to dip seven times in the river Jordan (2 Kings 5:10–14). But after the seventh dip he was healed and his skin was like that of a child.

- Moses must have felt like a fool when he led the children of Israel to a cul-de-sac in Egypt—when there was no way out—but was only told to "lift up your staff, and stretch out your hand over the sea and divide it" (Exod. 14:16). But the sea parted and the children of Israel crossed the Red Sea on dry land.

What will bring about the next great awakening is hundreds and hundreds of people who are unashamed of the Bible—they will fearlessly share the Gospel wherever they are—and who are unafraid to die.

The question is, How soon and how quickly will the next great awakening take place? It is my opinion that this will happen soon and suddenly. Whereas sometimes God works gradually, as He did in the first Great Awakening, as I mentioned earlier, Jonathan Edwards preached for several years—beginning in 1733—before the zenith of the New England Awakening came in 1741. America's second Great Awakening came suddenly—on August 6, 1801—and lasted less than a week! But its impact spread all over the South in a very short period of time. When king Hezekiah celebrated the Passover at a low spiritual ebb in the life of Israel, all were amazed that it came about "suddenly" (2 Chron.

29:36). The Holy Spirit fell "suddenly" on the Day of Pentecost. That is what I expect to happen now. With God all things are possible!

But there is more. After the writer of Hebrews told us to keep our eyes on Jesus, he told us to be aware of any bitterness in our hearts that may cause us to miss what God has in mind for us (Heb. 12:15). Bitterness and unforgiveness are identical twins. In much the same way Isaiah pointed out that the fast that pleases God is not merely praying and humbling ourselves (Isa. 58:5). It was to reach out to the poor, to cease quarreling with one another, and to stop "the pointing of the finger" (Isa. 58:9).

I see a day coming when there will be undoubted conversions by the thousands of university students. There will be conversions by the tens of thousands of millennials. There will be conversions of hundreds of thousands of African Americans. There will be millions of Muslims converted. It should not be surprising that the latter will cause the jealousy that Paul envisaged that would lead to the lifting of the blindness on Israel (Rom. 11:14).

Furthermore, as God said that royalty and "men of valor" would be turned over to Joshua, I expect to see high-profile people—those you would least expect to be slain by the power of the Spirit—to confess Jesus Christ as Lord and Savior openly. If God could strike down Saul of Tarsus on the road to Damascus by the Holy Spirit (Acts 9:4), He can save anybody. After all, if He could save you or me, He can save anybody.

What I see coming, then, is equal to the walls of Jericho falling. Yes. And do not forget that the nations to God "are like a drop from a bucket" (Isa. 40:15). America turning to God by hundreds and hundreds of thousands is her only hope and our only hope.

Finally, I have a recipe that I know will work if enough people listen to me and take the following seriously. In addition to prayer and standing on 2 Chronicles 7:14 is that if Christians everywhere from every denomination and every color—Evangelical, Charismatic, Roman Catholic, Asian, Hispanic, Black, and White—will forgive one another *totally*. That the pointing of the finger will come to an end.

I now share what I have taught all over the world. The greater the suffering, the greater the anointing; the greater the injustice, the greater the blessing that will come to those who forgive—totally.

Let us suppose for a moment that *you*, the reader of these lines, have been hurt more than anyone in your city. It could be that you were robbed, raped, lied about, abused as a child, or betrayed by your best friend. Perhaps your spouse was unfaithful to you, or you were promised a job but were betrayed. Maybe you have suffered incalculable injustices because of the color of your skin. Perhaps you were suspected or even convicted and imprisoned without a fair trial.

Did any of the above describe you? What if many of the above describe you?

The angels have a word for you: *Congratulations*! Yes. Because of what you have suffered you have a promise of blessing that no one around you has because they have not suffered as you have.

The promise of blessing is yours if you can totally forgive them.

My counsel, if you can accept it: instead of feeling sorry

for yourself (which I can fully understand) or vowing to get vengeance down the road, *let them off the hook—because of Jesus.*

If you could read the many letters I have received from those who did the impossible—like watching the walls of Jericho fall—namely, by totally forgiving the worst cruelty and injustice imaginable, you would be amazed. Seeing the joy that followed those who forgave totally—not to mention the blessing of God on them in many ways—you would very likely be motivated too, like these who overcame impossible odds by total forgiveness.

A Black lady I have never met made me almost famous in South Africa. All the major newspapers covered the story: she went to a prison to meet the White man who had ruthlessly murdered her parents. Reporters got ahold of the account of her being there and came to interview her. Why did she go to meet this person? Answer: she went there to forgive him. They asked her why. She said it was because my book *Total Forgiveness* had changed her life and made her want to forgive him.

This is why I say I have a recipe that I know will work. If I can persuade you, the reader—if there is someone out there you have not forgiven, I would plead with you to consider what I am saying in these lines.

I will tell you exactly why I believe this: it will be the nearest way I know to bring down the Holy Spirit on you. If you and many others will do this, you will have power to radiate Jesus and tell about Him like you have never before. It will make you fearless. Unashamed. Bold.

You would be obeying the Word—just like the children

of Israel did at Jericho. And when they did what they were commanded to do, "the wall fell down flat" (Josh. 6:20).

Jesus Christ is the same yesterday, today, and forever (Heb. 13:8). He promised never to leave you or forsake you (Heb. 13:5).

I urge you as humbly and lovingly as I know how, consider these words. You could truly be the key to the next great awakening.

And remember the words of the prophet Habakkuk:

> O LORD, I have heard the report of you, and your work, O LORD, do I fear. In the midst of the years revive it; in the mist of the years make it known; in wrath remember mercy.
>
> —HABAKKUK 3:2

CONCLUSION

I CLOSE WITH A story out of my life that I have told many times. In the darkest hour Louise and I have ever known, having been dealt an injustice I can never report to anyone as long as I live or after I die, Josif Tson from Romania turned up in my life. The providence of him being there at a particular moment turned out to be possibly the most pivotal time of my life. I die a thousand deaths at the thought of what life would be like had I not met him. Knowing that he would not tell anybody, I told Josif what "they" did, fully expecting him to put his arm around me and say, "R. T., get it out of your system—you ought to be angry." But instead, he said something to me for which I was not even remotely prepared. If I could narrow twenty-five years at Westminster Chapel down to fifteen minutes, the greatest moment is when Josif looked at me and said, "R. T., you must totally forgive them. Until you totally forgive them, you will be in chains. Release them, and you will be released."

No one had ever talked to me like that in my life. Faithful are the wounds of a friend. It is the hardest thing I have ever—ever—had to do. It will be the hardest thing you ever do. I still have to do it. The fallout of that time continues to this day. But the benefit that it was—*and still is*—to me is incalculable.

I will add, what was the worst moment of my life I now regard as the best moment of my life. God will do that for you too. I guarantee it. But on this condition: that you totally—*totally*—forgive them. Let them completely off the hook.

I promise this: you will never be sorry.

May the grace of almighty God—Father, Son, and Holy Spirit—be with you and abide with you now and forever. Amen.

NOTES

EPIGRAPH

1. Kieran Grogan, "Crossing Rivers," October 2007. Used with permission.

INTRODUCTION

1. Charles Creitz, "Cardinal Dolan Shares Pope Francis' Message for Coronavirus-Ravaged NYC," Fox News, April 16, 2020, https://www.foxnews.com/media/cardinal-dolan-pope-francis-message-nyc-coronavirus.
2. Katharine Lee Bates, "America the Beautiful," HymnTime.com, 1893, http://www.hymntime.com/tch/htm/o/b/f/obfsskis.htm.
3. John Newton, "I Saw One Hanging on a Tree," Hymnary.org, accessed July 23, 2020, https://hymnary.org/text/i_saw_one_hanging_on_a_tree_in_agony.

CHAPTER 1

1. Margaret J. Harris, "I Will Praise Him," Hymnary.org, accessed July 23, 2020, https://hymnary.org/text/when_i_saw_the_cleansing_fountain.

CHAPTER 3

1. Charles H. Spurgeon, "A Defense of Calvinism," The Spurgeon Archive, accessed July 23, 2020, https://archive.spurgeon.org/calvinis.php.
2. "Reagan the Man," Ronald Reagan Presidential Foundation and Institute, accessed July 23, 2020,

https://www.reaganfoundation.org/ronald-reagan/the-presidency/reagan-the-man/.

3. Helen Howarth Lemmel, "Turn Your Eyes Upon Jesus," Hymnary.org, 1922, https://hymnary.org/text/o_soul_are_you_weary_and_troubled.

CHAPTER 4

1. John Newton, "Amazing Grace! (How Sweet the Sound)," Hymnary.org, 1779, https://hymnary.org/text/amazing_grace_how_sweet_the_sound.

2. "John Newton, *Amazing Grace*," BaptistLife.com, accessed July 23, 2020, https://www.baptistlife.com/johnnewton.htm.

3. "7 Facts About Southern Baptists," Pew Research Center, June 7, 2019, https://www.pewresearch.org/fact-tank/2019/06/07/7-facts-about-southern-baptists/#:~:text=1The%20Southern%20Baptist%20Convention,Center's%202014%20Religious%20Landscape%20Study.&text=Southern%20Baptists%20make%20up%20about,U.S.%20evangelical%20Protestants%20(21%25).

4. "Abortion Statistics: United States Data and Trends," National Right to Life, accessed July 23, 2020, https://nrlc.org/uploads/factsheets/FS01AbortionintheUS.pdf.

5. "QuickFacts: California," US Census Bureau, July 1, 2019, https://www.census.gov/quickfacts/CA.

6. "QuickFacts: New York," US Census Bureau, July 1, 2019, https://www.census.gov/quickfacts/NY.

7. "C. S. Lewis Quotes," Goodreads, accessed July 23, 2020, https://www.goodreads.com/

quotes/733731-there-are-two-kinds-of-people-those-who-say-to.

CHAPTER 5

1. "Our History," Narramore Christian Foundation, accessed July 23, 2020, https://ncfliving.org/about_us/our-history.html.
2. Billy Graham, "Billy Graham: 'My Heart Aches for America,'" Billy Graham Evangelistic Association, July 19, 2012, https://billygraham.org/story/billy-graham-my-heart-aches-for-america/.

CHAPTER 6

1. "Charles Spurgeon Quotes," BrainyQuote, accessed July 23, 2020, https://www.brainyquote.com/quotes/charles_spurgeon_130021.
2. Frances Ridley Havergal, "Like a River Glorious," Hymnary.org, accessed July 23, 2020, https://hymnary.org/text/like_a_river_glorious
3. Bernard of Clairvaux, "Jesus, the Very Thought of Thee," Hymnary.org, accessed July 23, 2020, https://www.hymnal.net/en/hymn/h/209. Accessed July 21, 2020.
4. Newton, "Amazing Grace! (How Sweet the Sound)."

CHAPTER 7

1. William Williams, "Guide Me, O Thou Great Jehovah," Hymnary.org, accessed July 23, 2020, https://hymnary.org/hymn/AAHH2001/140.

2. Haldor Lillenas, "Come Over Into Canaan," Hymnary.org, accessed July 23, 2020, https://hymnary.org/text/why_wander_in_the_wilderness.
3. Markham W. Stackpole and Joseph N. Ashton, eds., Hymns for Schools and Colleges (Boston: Ginn and Company, 1913), https://tinyurl.com/y55snoed.

CHAPTER 9

1. "The Salvation Army North and South Carolina: 2016 Annual Report," The Salvation Army, accessed July 23, 2020, https://www.salvationarmycarolinas.org/about/story/impact-report-2016/.

CHAPTER 10

1. Isaac Watts, "When I Survey the Wondrous Cross," Hymnary.org, 1707, https://hymnary.org/text/when_i_survey_the_wondrous_cross_watts.

CHAPTER 11

1. William Cowper, "Breslau, LM," Hymnary.org, 1779, https://hymnary.org/text/what_various_hindrances_we_meet.